FAUSTO VICARELLI

KEYNES
THE INSTABILITY OF
CAPITALISM

UNIVERSITY OF PENNSYLVANIA PRESS
PHILADELPHIA 1984

850516

Original title: "Keynes, l'instabilità del capitalismo,"
Etas Libri, Milan, 1977.
Translation from Italian by John Richard Walker
The revised English edition benefited from partial financial
assistance from the C.N.R. under contract N.82.01201.10

Library of Congress Cataloging in Publication Data

Vicarelli, Fausto.
   Keynes: the instability of capitalism.

   (Post Keynesian economics)
   Translation of: Keynes, l'instabilità del capitalismo.
   Bibliography: p.
   Includes index.
   1. Keynesian economics. 2. Keynes, John Maynard,
1883–1946. 3. Capitalism. I. Title.
HB99.7.V5213   1984   330.15′6   83-14801
ISBN 0-8122-7914-X

Printed in the United States of America

To the Memory of
Professor Sidney Weintraub

CONTENTS

JOHN MAYNARD KEYNES

John Maynard Keynes lived from 1883 to 1946. His father was John Neville Keynes, a noted professor of logic and economics, himself the author of two excellent treatises (*Formal Logic*, 1884, and *The Scope and Method of Political Economy*, 1890) and the brilliant administrator and archivist of Cambridge University. His mother was Florence Ada Brown, a writer who also played a splendid role in promoting social works and institutions of national importance. Keynes was educated at Eton and moved on to King's, one of the most prestigious of the Cambridge colleges. He passed his youth at the very heart of British culture. A near contemporary at Cambridge, among many others to achieve great distinction later, was Bertrand Russell.[1]

The Keyneses' house was often visited by Cambridge scholars who were Neville's colleagues and friends. John Maynard thus grew up in the cultural atmosphere of a progressive society that was gradually breaking away from the rigid rules and traditions of the Victorian era. He was to mature in an exciting university atmosphere marked by new stimuli and achievements in science, literature, and social problems.

Keynes's relationship with political economy was "no love at first sight." He was admitted to Cambridge, at the end of 1901, as a student of "mathematics and classical literature." He pursued his studies in both disciplines with equal success but with differing degrees of enthusiasm. Despite his strong disposition toward mathematical philosophy, he found the study of mathematics somewhat difficult. In 1905 when he passed his exams, placing twelfth among

---

1. The great Russell, in his *Memoirs*, was to write that of all students Keynes had the most subtle and clear mind. See *The Autobiography of Bertrand Russell* (New York: Allen and Unwin, 1967).

the degree candidates in mathematics, he had not yet chosen his future profession. In the summer of the same year, however, he began to develop a passion for economics; he was fascinated in his readings by the original intellectual plight and later success of William Stanley Jevons; many years later, in 1936, he was to celebrate the centenary of Jevons's birth with particular warmth.[2]

While waiting to decide on a direction for his future career, Keynes attended the lectures given by Alfred Marshall, for long the most eminent of the Cambridge academic economists. Here Keynes came into contact with A. C. Pigou, who was shortly to succeed Marshall in the chair of political economy, and who was to become, in Keynes's view, a typical spokesman for that school of economic thought which Keynes was ultimately to attack—even denounce. Despite insistent suggestions from Marshall, who had intuitively apprehended his latent great abilities, Keynes could not bring himself to opt for a degree in economics. His eclecticism led him to several disciplines simultaneously, in particular, psychology and philosophy. He developed an abiding passion for the university debates on the themes then most in vogue and was disposed always toward an unequivocal stand in favor of or against the contesting positions and schools of thought.

By spring 1906 Keynes made the decision to abandon Cambridge and to prepare himself to join the civil service. By summer he scored handsomely in his exams and became assigned to the India Office. Yet his stay was brief. In 1908 Marshall, who was about to retire, offered Keynes a post as a reader in economics. Keynes accepted, and returned to Cambridge determined this time to commit himself to this new but not unfamiliar career, which was a family legacy.

It was immediately apparent that Keynes was not going to be content with the calm life of an ordinary academic economist. His Cambridge activities drove him to mingle with others. In time he was to add to his teaching and research the editorship of the *Economic Journal*, to become a renowned heavy financial investor, to act as a government adviser first in World War I and later as a British representative in all the most important international gather-

---

2. Keynes, "William Stanley Jevons," *Journal of the Royal Statistical Society* (1936), reprinted in *The Collected Writings of J. M. Keynes*, volumes published for the Royal Economic Society (London: Macmillan Press).

ings. This early intense fervor of activities was to culminate later in a still more intense stream of cultural interests, personal aspirations, and social enthusiasms enough to occupy many lifetimes.

The Life of John Maynard Keynes, written in 1951 by R. F. Harrod, nephew of the great Shakespearean Forbes Robertson, provides us with a splendid verbal portrait of the man of thought, poise, pose, reflection, and action. Only a person of nearly like stature, who had closely known Keynes's activities, who was an intimate and friend of his friends—and adversaries—and who had been part of the same culture and participated in like creative endeavors, could have sensed the salient features of such a rich, renowned, diverse, extraordinary personality. Harrod, once Keynes's pupil, intimate, associate, and constructive critic who knew every nuance of the man for more than twenty years, was admirably equipped for the task, for he was himself one of the most original of economists, who could measure genius with his own credo of detachment, integrity, and perception. No other work on Keynes could bear the stamp of so personal a recollection.[3]

It would be presumptuous of me to conceive of my work as "competing" with Harrod's in a biographical way. My aim is quite different. This study is a quest for the tracks laid by Keynes in economics, from the novitiate to the commanding figure he became. It is a supplement, a complement to the Harrod portrait and is intended for economists as well as for a wider, nonprofessional audience.

---

3. For a more informal and casual, but always informative and enlightening study, see the small volume by D. E. Moggridge, ed., Keynes—Aspects of the Man and His Work (London: Macmillan, 1974).

INTRODUCTION

Probably no economist has ever been involved as intensely in the economic problems of his time, or in all their diversity and range, as Keynes. His participation in domestic and international economic matters reflected his character. He was a man who assumed a personal commitment to argue forcibly his opinion on any question he deemed of importance to his country or to good and harmonious international relations.

The range of this commitment undoubtedly derived from his privileged intellectual background and was in part a result of the historical period that confronted him. Few periods could have offered more opportunities to analyze the workings, advantages, and limitations of the capitalist economic system than the years between 1910 and 1946. The British decision to abandon the gold standard on the outbreak of World War I, the economic negotiations of the Paris Peace Talks, the "return to gold" halfway through the 1920s, the Great Depression of the 1930s, the shattering devastation of World War II, and then the unparalleled opportunities for the setting up of a new international monetary system once peace returned: a historical concatenation of events as profound as these could hardly have failed to incite a mind such as Keynes's to identify the key mechanisms in the workings of a market economy and thus

A previous draft of my manuscript was read by P. Ciocca and by C. Gnesutta, J. Kregel, S. Parrinello, and S. Weintraub to whom I am indebted for a number of constructive observations which helped enormously to improve the final version. I want to thank in particular Professor Weintraub for his valuable and generous help in the preparation of the English edition of the book. He and the others who helped are absolved of any failings; responsibility for the final version is of course my own.

indirectly to seize on the possible flaws and chinks that could lead these mechanisms to falter and even fail.

Keynes's intellectual legacy was huge. His writings range from an important contribution to the logical foundations of the calculus of probability (*A Treatise on Probability*, 1921) to a lucid analysis of Indian monetary and financial institutions (*Indian Currency and Finance*, 1913) and of the British financial system on the eve of the First World War (1914). Included is his more or less merciless attack on the political follies in economic policy perpetrated by the Allies at the Paris Peace Conference (*The Economic Consequences of the Peace*, 1919) and those committed by the British government in its ill-advised "return to gold" (*The Economic Consequences of Mr. Churchill*, 1925). Dwelling aside but finally to be pushed on to center stage are his fundamental works of economic theory (*A Tract on Monetary Reform*, 1923; *A Treatise on Money*, 1930; and *The General Theory of Employment, Interest, and Money*, 1936).

Keynes is considered the founder of modern macro-economic thought, though the name itself seems to derive from Erik Lindahl. Although nearly a half-century has elapsed since the publication of the *General Theory*, its significance and vitality still remain controversial; it unquestionably marked a break, as a breath of fresh air, from the consolidated theoretical tradition, and from the contemporary systemic approaches to the analysis of economic reality. Given its timing in the midst of market capitalism's most traumatic unemployment tragedy in the modern century—and Keynes's own considered verdict on his accomplishment—the *General Theory* must be assigned the top priority as the definitive systematization of Keynes's theoretical thinking. It emerged as the final published statement in a vigorous yet tormented intellectual process, the legacy of a process during which Keynes was not afraid to alter course when he felt he had been led by his own reasoning to a cul-de-sac.

J. A. Schumpeter, referring specifically to Keynes, offered this not unsympathetic assessment carrying some ameliorating judgment:

> Every comprehensive "theory" of an economic state of society consists of two complementary but essentially distinct elements. There is, first, the theorist's view about the basic features of that state of society, about what is and what is not important in order to understand its life at a given time. Let us call this his vision. And there is,

second, the theorist's technique, an apparatus by which he concep-
tualizes his vision and which turns the latter into concrete propositions or "theories."[1]

That Schumpeter chose to illustrate his well-considered proposition in a judgment aimed in specific reference to Keynes was no
coincidence. What vision did Keynes form of capitalism through his
confrontation with the concrete problems of his time? What lines
did he follow when he translated this vision into theoretical propositions? Were they necessarily of general validity when they finally
coalesced in the *General Theory*? What was the logic animating his
brilliant intuitions, his sometimes nonlinear views, his contradictions, occasional self-doubts, and the at times obscure or elliptical
reasoning which eventually clothed the body of thought behind the
General Theory to give it worldly form and fame?

My aim here is to ponder the answers to these questions in
terms accessible to a nonspecialist public. This will entail sifting
through an often confused mass of academic literature generated by
forty years of "interpreting" Keynes. Until recently any attempt to
make order out of chaos, at least by the quantitative measure, would
have appeared impossible.

The Royal Economic Society's recent publication of Keynes's
complete works has opened a rich and hitherto inaccessible mine
containing the whole of Keynes's published writings, and including
the available part of his enormous correspondence.[2] This open cor-
ridor has greatly encouraged me to think that a lode could be extracted by some manageable digging. Above all I have been
heartened by a conviction that Keynes would have wanted many of
his unpublished and lesser-known writings to be widely circulated,
rather than suppressed—unlike Adam Smith who preferred that
his literary remains be destroyed. There is, for one thing, the clos-
ing passage of Harrod's *Life*:

> It was some two years after his death that I found myself lying
> outstretched one beautiful summer day on a slope of the Sussex

---

1. J. A. Schumpeter, *Ten Great Economists from Marx to Keynes*
(London: G. Allen and Unwin, 1952), p. 268.
2. *The Collected Writings of J. M. Keynes*, volumes published for
the Royal Economic Society (London: Macmillan Press). Cited hereafter
as *C.W.K.*

Downs. High above me, seated on a fine white horse, was the handsome one-armed shepherd, now turned cowherd, Beckett Standon. He was talking with rural fluency about the herd, explaining how the farm had become self-supporting in feeding-stuffs, and describing Keynes' plans for its improvement and extension. He evidently knew something about high politics also. "His Lordship would never have approved the way they frittered away that American Loan." There was a pause in the flow, and his face grew a shade more serious; he was seeking the right words. "But apart from alla that," he said, "you know that he was a *good* man; he'd sit on the edge of a stack and talk to me for a long time about things—very homely."[3]

---

3. R. F. Harrod, *The Life of John Maynard Keynes* (London: Macmillan, 1951), p. 650.

PART I

TOWARD A VISION
OF CAPITALISM

CHAPTER 1

THE INDIAN MONETARY SYSTEM
AND THE ROLE
OF FINANCIAL INSTITUTIONS

The first part of this book will outline Keynes's vision of capitalism, that is, his specific ideas of the basic features of an economic system based on free enterprise and on private capital accumulation. A vision of capitalism, in Schumpeter's sense, implies an intuitive grasp of its key points, which in turn implies that certain economic phenomena are seen as of primary and others as of secondary importance in the logic underlying the historical evolution of capitalism as an operative system.

Apart from the *Treatise on Probability*, a large proportion of Keynes's earlier intellectual energies prior to his major theoretical works—*A Treatise on Money* and *The General Theory*—were devoted to current problems arising from often dramatic historical events. He seemed to rely more on objective observation, good sense, and rigorous inductive logic than on the orthodox Marshallian theory he had learned from his academic studies. It did not matter whether he was dealing with the workings of the Indian monetary system, European reconstruction after World War I, or Britain's "return to gold" in the 1920s. In each of the problems and situations that he analyzed, Keynes displayed an enviable ability to identify basic causes and thence to draw conclusions of general validity for the understanding of capitalism. Compared to traditional economic theory, permeated with its abstract concepts and cautions engendered by "marginalist" economics, this was a revolutionary way of attacking reality. In retrospect it is easy to see the need that Keynes felt to reconstruct a theory that corresponded to the view of reality he detected.

The *Treatise on Money* and *The General Theory* were both responses to this need and assaults on the dominant theory. It therefore seems that one perspective for interpreting Keynes's contribution and evaluating its relevance to contemporary problems is to start with his view of capitalism. Much of the massive interpretative literature has generally been compromised by completely abstracting his *Treatise* and *General Theory* from the earthly context in which they were generated. An alternative approach is the only way to avoid a disembodied caricature of his contribution to economic theory.

Keynes's first contact with concrete disarray in the economic world came through his work at the India Office. His two years there provided an opportunity to look into certain aspects of Indian institutions, especially the financial and monetary system.

India's monetary and financial problems and their relation to the workings of the British monetary system had been at the center of government and public concern for some years before Keynes in 1910 was invited to give six lectures on Indian finance at the London School of Economics. The knowledge acquired at the India Office, together with the material collected for these lectures, formed the basis for a future lecture on the same subject to the Royal Economic Society in 1911. Two years later, after some further research and a deeper refinement of the problem, Keynes published his *Indian Currency and Finance*.

It was his first book. The whole issue was at the center of a stormy campaign which an anonymous correspondent had promoted in the letter column of the *Times*. A lukewarm reception was precluded. The book would be either a smashing success or a resounding failure. It was a success. In the same year that the book appeared Keynes had been invited to participate on a Royal Commission mandated to investigate the Indian monetary system and the role of the India Office. The clarity and the calm with which he untangled the intricate operations of the Indian monetary system, and the confident thrust of his advocacy of his views concerning the general direction of reform, won over the commission. Although the commission exercised pains not to appear unduly influenced by Keynes's book, the chairman, Austen Chamberlain, acknowledged publicly that the final report did not depart from the main lines of the book.

Although Keynes's specific focus was on the economic and institutional order underlying the Indian monetary system, *Indian Currency and Finance* also contained broad-ranging observations on the characteristics and advantages and disadvantages of the gold standard and the gold exchange standard. The domestic and international monetary events buffeting the majority of countries over the previous twenty years, following the wide-spread abandonment of bimetallism, could all be explained in terms of the functioning of these two basic types of system. In this setting we are thus able to catch some first impressions of Keynes's analysis of capitalism and expose his attitude on the importance of monetary and financial affairs.

It is useful to recall the essential characteristics of the Indian financial and monetary system. Throughout the second half of the nineteenth century, and at the time Keynes was writing, the Indian monetary system was centered on the silver rupee. Up until 1893 the public had been free to turn its silver into coin at the mint. The value of the rupee, expressed in gold, had thus fluctuated in line with the gold value of silver ingots. The decision to end the free coining of silver by the mint had been taken in pursuance to the continual depreciation of the gold value of silver, which meant a steady fall in the external value of the rupee, with the typical result of encouraging exports and increasing domestic prices.

In the same legislation, passed in 1893, the Indian government committed itself to exchange sterling into rupees at a rate of one to fifteen; no commitment was made, however, to exchange rupees into sterling. In other words, the Indian authorities fixed the maximum value of the rupee in terms of the pound but did not fix a minimum value. What they did do over the following years was to reduce government minting of rupees, the aim being to improve the exchange rate vis-à-vis sterling. In 1898 a special commission (the Fowler Commission) was set up to study the possibility of introducing a gold-based system; the reduced minting of coin had led to a spontaneous appreciation of the rupee, which reached 1s 4d or some fifteen rupees to the pound. This made it easier, a year later, to implement the first part of the commission's proposals and thus render British currency convertible into Indian legal tender at a rate of one sovereign for fifteen rupees.

The long-term objective of the Fowler Commission was, however, more ambitious, namely, the introduction of a new gold coin, minted in India, to circulate side by side with the rupee as a means of exchange for general public use. The proposals put forward by the Indian government, and the India Office, to open an offshoot of the British mint in Bombay to coin gold, were rejected outright by the British Treasury. In 1903 the whole project was thus abandoned despite a number of attempts to introduce gold coin into circulation. Keynes recalled the effort made in 1900 and 1901 when the post offices and the banking system were used to inject 6.75 million sterling worth of gold coin into the system. The Indian public was unaccustomed to using gold coin as a means of exchange; the value of the sovereign was too high for a poor country such as India. Being inconvenient in circulation, the coins ended up being exported or returned to the government in the form of payments by private citizens to the public administration. Keynes invoked a widely held view in British financial opinion when he observed that the enormous accumulation of gold by the Indian public was consistent with an Indian aversion to the use of gold as money. There was the fact that the mass of this metal was hoarded, used as jewelry or ornaments or even as medicine. The persistence of non-money demand for gold was ample confirmation of a hostility to money usage.

The range of different forms of money in circulation was completed by banknotes, in denominations ranging from 5 to 10,000 rupees, regularly issued by the Indian government in exchange for silver rupees, British gold coin, or gold ingots. For this purpose India was divided into a series of different zones corresponding more or less to the main provinces. For a long time banknotes were legal tender payable to the bearer only within the zone where they had been issued. This strange rule was imposed by virtue of the fear that with a public unused to holding banknotes, and a strongly seasonal pattern of payments, requests for conversion would be concentrated in a limited number of centers and at specific times of the year. The outcome, however, was to discourage the spread of this particular means of payment. After 1903 small denomination banknotes were freed from these geographic constraints and by 1911, 10, 50, and 100 rupee notes were recognized as legal tender throughout India. Subsequently the volume of banknotes in circulation increased considerably.

The reserves of various origin, held by the Indian authorities as backing for the currency in circulation, were kept separate. Those formed through the minting of rupees were known as *gold standard* reserves; those created through the issuance of banknotes were considered *paper currency* reserves.[1] The former were ordinarily invested in British gilt-edged stock denominated in sterling, while the latter were also held in bonds, denominated either in sterling or in rupees, but only up to a predetermined ceiling. The remaining reserves consisted of gold and silver ingots, rupees, or sovereigns. The government could also draw on its cash balances fed from treasury revenue, and consisting of both rupees and sterling.

The volume and composition of these reserves had to be such as to always allow the government to meet its commitment to pay rupees in exchange for banknotes and sovereigns, and to supply sovereigns in exchange for rupees. In reality, as already mentioned, the Indian authorities were under no obligation to offer sovereigns for rupees at a predetermined exchange rate. In practice, however, its policy was to defend the gold value of 1s 4d per rupee, reached in 1898. Technically speaking, fluctuations in the exchange rate of the rupee against sterling were controlled through the sale of so-called Council bills. These were denominated in sterling available in London but were payable in rupees in India. A British importer could purchase these bills and use them as a means of payment to an Indian exporter. The Indian government's commitment to sell rupees at an exchange rate of 1s 4d automatically prevented Council bills from exceeding that price by more than the cost of transferring sovereigns from Britain to India; otherwise, British importers would find it to their advantage to pay directly in India with gold. On the other hand, the only circumstance in which Council bills could fall below the price by more than the cost of the transfer would be if it became impossible to transfer gold from India to Britain. For a short period, at the end of 1907, a balance of payments crisis led the Indian authorities to hinder the export of gold. As a result the value of the rupee fell by more than would have otherwise been expected.

The Indian system, Keynes observed, had all the features of a gold-exchange standard: (1) gold coin represented only a negligible

---

1. Whereas the issuing of a banknote led to an increase in the reserves equivalent to the number of rupees, silver or gold, paid by the bearer, the increase in reserves, when silver rupees were coined, was limited to the difference between the face value of the coin and the intrinsic value of the metal coined.

proportion of domestic means of payment; (2) the local currency was not necessarily convertible into gold; (3) the authorities were committed, at least at an administrative level, to controlling the external value of the local currency; and (4) a significant proportion of reserves consisted of claims on foreign assets.

The characteristic structure of the Indian financial and monetary system had come into being only gradually, as a result of a series of measures taken by the Indian government, and not always as the result of a coherent line of policy. At times there was friction with the British authorities. Nonetheless, the gold-exchange standard had been adopted by many countries in Europe and, following the Indian example, in Asia. The captivating line was: Why try to force the system toward a gold standard in which gold acted as a means of payment both domestically and internationally when the only flexibility enjoyed by the monetary authorities either way was the ultimate ability to manipulate bank rate?

This was no mere rhetorical question. In *Indian Currency and Finance* Keynes posed the problem in such a way as to inject an almost deliberate provocation. His target was those whose views were echoed in the debate in the *Times*, and according to whom it was high time that India adopted gold as its main medium of exchange and brought the Indian financial and monetary system into line with the British gold standard model. What Keynes had to beat was the idea that the free circulation of gold was a kind of deus ex machina capable of insuring domestic and international monetary tranquillity. Undoubtedly, this idea descended from David Hume's theory, published in 1752, on the movement of gold.[2] As is well known, Hume presented a theory of the "specie flow mechanism," according to which, under a universal gold standard, a deficit in a given country's balance of trade automatically sets in motion a rebalancing adaptive mechanism: gold flows from the country in deficit to the country in surplus. On the basis of the quantity theory of money, this should lead to a fall in the general price level in the former country and an increase in the latter; this in turn should foster a compensatory shift in trade.

The specie mechanism that Hume elaborated stemmed from at least two fundamental assumptions: (1) the validity of the quan-

---

2. *On the Balance of Trade* (1752); reprinted in Hume, *Writings on Economics*, ed. E. Rotwein (Edinburgh: Nelson, 1955).

tity theory of money, and (2) the absence of both capital movements and any interventionist authority capable of implementing contrary goals of monetary policy. Certainly neither the financial circles calling for a gold standard for India, nor even Keynes himself, took issue with the first of these assumptions. As for the second assumption, opinion had it as decidedly unrealistic. While it would be naive to claim that the conventional wisdom maintained the crude, undiluted theory of gold movements in its original form, it was nevertheless accepted that even allowing for the monetary authorities' ability to manipulate bank rate, Hume's theory remained valid. A country in deficit could only halt the drain of gold by increasing the domestic rate of interest, thereby attracting an inflow of capital, or at least slowing the outflow.

As Keynes saw it, the manipulation of interest rates was not a generally valid means of halting an outflow of gold. Increases in domestic interest rates are only effective in countries with a strong and well-organized capital market. Moreover, this response is faster and more credible in creditor countries who are the net exporters of capital. In the absence of an efficient capital market, the central bank, in his opinion, should hold claims on foreign assets for ready use in periods of crisis. In this way the bank avoids bearing the cost of an excessive accumulation of non-interest-bearing reserves.

Two additional conditions had to be met if this mechanism was to guarantee a certain degree of stability: (1) the domestic currency should not be tied to gold, and (2) its exchange rate against an international currency should be allowed at least some (minor) fluctuation. The first of these conditions was particularly essential in that it allowed the monetary authorities to amass the country's gold reserves in their own hands rather than dispersing them in the hands of the public. These are, in fact, the essential characteristics of a gold-exchange standard.

It follows from these considerations that it is impossible to give an a priori definition of an "ideal" monetary system for all varieties of essentially capitalistic economies. Rather, one has to weigh the state of development of a specific country's financial institutions and in particular the structural aspects and international role of its capital market. The British example, Keynes thought, was deceptive. The fact that Britain had succeeded over the previous half century in maintaining a certain degree of monetary stability was not due to its operating on the gold standard as such but rather to Britain's commanding economic position with regard to the rest of the world, to its particular position vis-à-vis the members of the British Empire, and above all to the strategic role of the "City" in the world financial market.

It was also misleading to concentrate attention on the circulation of gold coin in Britain; the majority of transactions used checks, whose circulation was growing continuously. This, in fact, was the banking system's reaction to the restrictions on the issuing of banknotes, imposed by law as far back as 1844. The British banking system, Keynes observed, had managed to reestablish a degree of elasticity in the money supply which an over-restrictive law had attempted to abolish. The efficiency, ingenuity, and vitality of the banking system thus constituted a further pillar for the stability of the monetary system. It was hard to visualize the British system without the stern presence of the Bank of England as "lender of last resort." In the Indian monetary system, on the other hand, there was no central bank. This, and not the lack of a domestic gold currency, was the shortcoming on which attention should have seized.

The most serious consequence of the lack of a central bank in India was a highly "inelastic" money supply. While only the state could issue banknotes, the volume issued could only increase if there were a parallel increase in reserves of precious metals. Thus any increase in the money supply depended on the imports of sovereigns from London. This rendered the Indian monetary system heavily dependent on financial conditions in the City and significantly raised interest rates, a precondition for movements of funds between two such distant markets.

With the same level of reserves, a central bank capable of manipulating the issuing of notes by varying the volume of bills discounted to the banking system would have made it possible for the money supply to adapt to fluctuations in demand. But in India it was not even possible to use variations in the volume of checks as a buffer against seasonal fluctuations in the demand for money; their use had yet to become a conventional public habit.

Keynes insisted that the lack of a central bank also had a further consequence disturbing the smooth functioning of a monetary system: this was the problem of reserve management. In the Indian system the government was forced to hold back a volume of reserves sufficient not only to block any plausible crisis in the balance of payments but also to support the banks when faced with a domestic crisis of confidence leading to a run on deposits. Consequently, despite the government's inability to control the money in the hands of the banks, it had to fortify itself with reserves for them as well as for itself. At the same time, there was the need for forecasts of the state of the government's reserves which partly depended on trends in its own revenues and expenditures, or its cash balances, and thus on government budgetary policy. The use of the reserves to make loans to the banks thus created confusing signals on budgetary and credit policy, or in modern jargon, on fiscal and monetary policy. Keynes believed such loans to banks were dangerous, though in the absence of a central bank, they were probably a lesser evil than the ready alternatives.

Finally, one last circumstance that had to be borne in mind was that the only banks in India allowed to engage in foreign operations were a group known as the exchange banks. These discounted Indian exporters' bills of credit while at the same time their London subsidiaries sold Council bills to British importers. In practice, these banks had complete dominance in the financing of foreign trade. Curbing them entirely was impossible; it was not even known what proportion of their deposits was held in India and how much in London.

Keynes was just thirty years old when he published *Indian Currency and Finance*, and this was his first attempt at systematic economic policy analysis. Nonetheless, from his examination of a current problem pertaining to a specific historical period—the debate on the Indian monetary system—he was able to extract a series of conclusions of general importance, even to market economies today. On the two typical monetary systems of his period, the gold standard and the gold exchange standard, his judgment that the prevalent system in the future would be the gold exchange standard contained the remarkable intuition that although gold was destined to disappear as a commonplace international means of exchange it would linger on as an almost indispensable reference point in international payments. Keynes insisted that monetary systems had to be evaluated in relation to the prevailing economic and financial institutions and the socioeconomic conditions with which they had to operate. When Rothschild stated that it was impossible to have a gold standard without a gold currency, Keynes replied caustically: "Financiers of this type will not admit the feasibility of anything until it has been demonstrated to them by practical experience" (pp. 24–25). All this seemed a premonition of the irrational return to gold in the 1920s, and an embryonic statement of the principles that were to dictate his position at Bretton Woods, some thirty years later.

As far as the setting up of an Indian central bank was concerned, Keynes presented the Chamberlain Commission with a memorandum.[3] Here he broadened the general line of argument he had used in *Indian Currency and Finance* and summed it up in a list of "advantages" and "criticisms" in which the former were out of all proportion to the latter. Keynes's point of view did not win acceptance; the publication of his memorandum as an appendix to the commission's final report was an act of pure courtesy. This, however, simply made Keynes's position more intriguing. In a system in which there was no longer any argument about the central bank's "right" to play an active role, should there be a clear separation between policy matters reserved for the Treasury and those concerned by the bank's management of money supply?

At first sight, Keynes's arguments in support of an independent role for the central bank in monetary management appear to be dictated by pragmatic considerations of efficiency; his defense seems merely technical. In the same way as when he was considering the best kind of standard from a domestic and international point of view, he does not pose fundamental tenets concerning the role of finance in capitalist development; still less does he question the legitimacy of capitalism itself. Nonetheless, it would be superficial to consider the first of Keynes's serious works as merely "technicalities for technicians." My own view is that *Indian Currency and Finance* represents the first phase in Keynes's awakening to the way in which capitalism works. It can be likened to the first frame in Keynes's personal vision of the mechanism that allows the system to function.

It did not escape Keynes that India's intricate monetary affairs and the pressures that had led to the definition of the rules governing her monetary and financial system reflected the struggle between opposing interests. He noted, for example, how for a long time the stabilization of the rupee's value in gold had been hin-

---

3. *Memorandum on Proposals for the Establishment of a State Bank in India* (1913); reprinted in *C.W.K.* 15:151–214.

dered by the argument that gradual currency devaluation was essential for the growth of Indian exports, observing how the vested exporter interests which had benefited from devaluation contrasted with the general well-being of the community, which was condemned to suffer persistent inflation (pp. 1–2). Concerning the accumulation of gold in India Keynes wrote:

> It is interesting to reflect that India's love of the precious metals, ruinous though it has been to her own economic development, has flourished in the past to the great advantage of Western nations. Every one knows Jevons's description of India as the sink of the precious metals, always ready to absorb the redundant bullion of the West and to save Europe from the more violent disturbances to her price level. In very recent years, while the South African mines have been reaching the zenith of their production, she has been fulfilling to perfection her role of sink. Prices have been rising, as it is, much faster than is healthy and in a way very disadvantageous to such a creditor nation as Great Britain, to whom large sums fixed in terms of gold are annually due. It is reasonable to think that without the assistance of the Indian demand, they would have risen still faster. (P. 70)

Keynes's awareness of what lay behind the technical curtain did not distract him from identifying the nerve centers, upon whose working depended the orderly development of capitalism. If the widespread use of gold as a domestic currency leads to a dispersion of reserves, and in the process destabilizes a country's monetary system with inevitable consequences for foreign trade, and thus on other world economies, then there is nothing to be gained and everything to be lost by adopting a gold standard. If the accumulation of metal in quantities that are in excess of reasonable forecasts of needs becomes itself an obstacle to economic growth, or if the absence of a central bank forces the state to lend money to the banks and thus involves itself with interests whose aims and rules are different from its own, would not the removal of these distortions be a good thing?

One might argue that although Keynes had acquired a degree of wisdom about the non-neutrality of financial institutions and money vis-à-vis the interests directly engaged in the organization of a capitalist economy, his steadfast rationale was to improve the efficiency of these institutions. In a deep sense, despite a vast ideological gulf, his welfare principle for society was in some ways similar to the optimum of Vilfredo Pareto. Keynes needed no convincing that the general interest would be enhanced by reforms that would eliminate generally damaging inefficiencies.

CHAPTER 2

THE PARIS PEACE CONFERENCE: EUROPEAN RECONSTRUCTION AND THE FRAGILITY OF THE CAPITALIST ACCUMULATION PROCESS

The First World War saw Keynes heavily engaged in serving his country as a civil servant at the Treasury. His teaching load and research at Cambridge, and the editorship of the *Economic Journal*, which he had assumed in 1912, would have been enough to fill a normal working day. Early in 1915 he nonetheless agreed to become assistant to Sir G. Paish, special adviser to David Lloyd George, who at that time was chancellor of the Exchequer. Teaching and theoretical research were obviously not enough to satisfy his passion to match himself in concrete economic problems or to satisfy a need he may well have felt to make a sacrifice for the nation by applying his professional talents in those sectors where they could prove most useful.[1]

After an initial period in which he worked as secretary to a commission for wheat, Keynes joined Number 1 Division in the Treasury, which was preoccupied with finance. Here he assisted Reginald McKenna, the new chancellor of the Exchequer, in all the most important and unexpected hurdles thrown up in a war economy. During the last two years of hostilities he had a more presti-

---

1. His moral refusal to even register for conscription is well known, even though he was most unlikely to be called up. See Harrod, *Life*, pp. 214–15.

gious and responsible role as head of Division A, concerned with delicate sensitivities of inter-Allied finance, and in particular the knotted financial relations with the United States.

In November 1918 Germany and the Allies signed the armistice, attesting the German government's complete and unconditional acceptance of President Woodrow Wilson's Fourteen Points and later clarifications. These were, in fact, the peace conditions that Wilson had laid down in a message to the American Congress in January 1918 and in four subsequent speeches. The American president's general peace principles had been accepted by the other Allies, with the addition of two specifications concerning the freedom of the seas and the matter of war reparations. Unfortunately, these ideas were expressed in abstract declarations and resounding statements of good intent. Any translation of the conditions into a detailed agreement—a peace treaty proper—would require much in subtle international diplomacy which had not yet begun.

At the beginning of 1919 the delegations from the main belligerents prepared to meet in Paris to open the peace conference conceived to give birth to the treaty. It was to be a difficult and painful delivery. Although Keynes was tapped to play an active off-stage role, he was unable to influence the course of events in the way he thought it should go.

Keynes was initially charged with responsibility as the leading representative of the Treasury on the British delegation. From February 1919 on he also served on the Supreme Economic Council as the official representative of Austen Chamberlain, the then chancellor of the Exchequer in Lloyd George's new government. He was also one of the two British Empire representatives on the conference's finance committee and president of the financial delegates in the armistice negotiations with Germany.

Keynes arrived in Paris on 10 January 1919. On 14 January he was already able to inform London of the excellent results of his talks about new loans for Britain with Norman Davis, the American Treasury representative. Given the previous American attitude, mainly rejection had been expected. Satisfaction with this immediate personal success was not enough, however, to dissipate Keynes's first distinct impressions of a cold and hostile atmosphere in relations between the different delegations, especially the clearly oppressive and revanchist French attitude toward the Germans. In a memoir written some years later and published posthumously in

1949, Keynes was to give an admirable account of the personalities of those involved in the setting of one of the early meetings at Treves. The picture that emerges from *Dr. Melchior: A Defeated Enemy* gives us a clearer impression of the forces that were to shape the proceedings of the conference: the Allies' conflicting interests; the steadfast French goal of wrecking forever a prospective German war economy. It is thus worthwhile examining this memoir in a little greater detail.[2]

Dr. Carl Melchior, to whom the article was dedicated, led the German financial delegation. He and Keynes were to become friends and this friendship was later extended to their respective families. The Treves meeting was the first of many in this small German town, the immediate aim being to assess available German food supplies. As a result of the "blockade," which the Allies had prolonged even after the armistice, Germany was in fact unable to acquire food abroad. Although the armistice formally allowed Germany to import sufficient food to meet her needs, French finance minister Klotz held to the position that not a gram of gold should be allowed to leave Germany for purchases abroad. The breach widened, and Klotz later became an open enemy of Keynes. In 1924 he wrote to the *Times* charging Keynes with megalomania.

President Wilson had solemnly declared that "so long as hunger continued to gnaw the foundations of government would continue to crumble," expressing his trust that "the French Finance Department would withdraw their objection, as we were faced with the great problems of Bolshevism and the forces of dissolution which now threatened society." Klotz, however, had replied that it was not just a matter of food but also of justice: Why should Germany use her gold reserves to buy food instead of paying for the damage she had done during the war?

The dispute was further complicated by the fact that the Allies had agreed not to renew the armistice if Germany was not prepared to cede her merchant navy. Short of tonnage as a result of sinkings by German submarines, the Allies set up a clamor for the German fleet immediately; the writing of an appropriate clause into the peace treaty could come later. The Germans, on the other hand, were reluctant to transfer ships that could be a precious bargaining counter

---

2. Published posthumously under the title *Two Memoirs*, ed. Rupert Hart-Davis; reprinted in *C.W.K.* 10:389–429.

in the coming negotiations. More to the point, they wanted an American loan to purchase food abroad.

Keynes was convinced that the blockade should be lifted immediately, and that the French adamancy was absurd. He thus attempted, in informal conversations as well as officially, to convince Melchior to soften the German stand on ship tonnage. In return, he hoped that the French would adopt a more reasonable attitude over the sequence of payment for supplies. If the deal succeeded it would be possible to send food immediately, and to talk about payment later. In this way Wilson's solemn declaration could be translated into concrete action. But was the great American willingness to supply food a genuine consequence of the president's generosity? The president was sincere, Keynes argued, but at the same time he also had to deal with an excess production of pigs that was a result of the price support policy adopted by Hoover, who had been in charge of food during the war. Quoting an extract from a report he had sent to the chancellor of the Exchequer, Keynes added a further stroke to his picture:

> As regards bacon, it has been suggested by the Americans that we unload on Germany the large stocks of low-grade bacon which we now hold, and replace these by fresher stocks from America which would be more readily saleable. From the food point of view this would clearly be a good deal for us. . . . The situation is a curious one. The blockade on fats to neutral countries is being raised, and Germany is to receive fat supplies on a very generous scale. Bolshevism is to be defeated and the new era to begin. At the Supreme War Council, President Wilson was very eloquent on the subject of instant action on these lines. But really the underlying motive of the whole thing is Mr Hoover's abundant stocks of low-grade pig products at high prices which must at all costs be unloaded on someone, enemies failing Allies. When Mr Hoover sleeps at night visions of pigs float across his bedclothes and he frankly admits that at all hazards the nightmare must be dissipated.[3]

The Treves meetings were only the first carbine skirmishes in a long-distance artillery duel. For several months the opposed delegations at Paris were to move back and forth across a treacherous bog of compromise and vested interest. The really heavy fighting

---

3. Ibid., pp. 398–99.

was within the Allied camp. Each of the four main victor countries tried to deflect the conference in a direction most favorable to itself. The only role left to the Germans was to make their observations on a treaty already drawn up, beforehand. The Allies' differing positions were already clear. France and Italy were seeking to obtain as much as possible of the residue of German riches; Britain wanted to oppose French and German demands insofar as these were damaging to British interests. Apart from declarations of principle, the United States had no clear policy at all and in the end accepted the decisions agreed upon by the other Allies. In the Council of Four formed by Georges Clemenceau, Lloyd George, Wilson, and Vittorio Orlando, it was the French prime minister who dominated the stage:

> Clemenceau was by far the most eminent member of the Council of Four, and he had taken the measure of his colleagues. He alone both had an idea and had considered it in all its consequences. His age, his character, his wit, and his appearance joined to give him objectivity and a defined outline in an environment of confusion. One could not despise Clemenceau or dislike him, but only take a different view as to the nature of civilised man, or indulge, at least, a different hope.[4]

Among the many problems under discussion two were of fundamental importance if the conference was to achieve solutions compatible with European economic recovery and German survival, namely, inter-Allied debts and German reparations. Keynes applied himself diligently to the struggle for a feasible solution. He strove valiantly to convince the French—and Lloyd George—that it was absurd to claim that Germany should pay reparations which even included war pensions and subsidies paid by the Allies to their own citizens. His pleas however were in vain. After the American rejection of a scheme based on cancelling inter-Allied debts, he prepared an option for issuing Treasury bills by Germany and her allies, to bear an interest rate of 4 percent and jointly guaranteed by the issuing countries and the Allies. The Americans were unwilling to accede to even this proposal. In a letter dated 3 May 1919, President Wilson informed Lloyd George, explaining the

---

4. *The Economic Consequences of the Peace* (London: Macmillan, 1919); reprinted in *C.W.K.* 2:18.

American rejection: "It would not be possible for me to secure from
the Congress of the United States authority to place a Federal guarantee upon bonds of European origin."[5] To Keynes the letter appeared as a non sequitur, even a personal affront:

> You have suggested that we all address ourselves to the problem of
> helping to put Germany on her feet, but how can your experts or
> ours be expected to work out a *new* plan to furnish working capital
> to Germany when we deliberately start out by taking away all Ger-
> many's *present* capital?[6]

After a further round of discussions to induce the Council of
Four to draft an emergency plan for Europe, Keynes decided to
resign. He had despaired of exerting a positive influence over the
decisions taken by the Great Four. At the same time he felt an ever
stronger urge to be free to denounce to the world the mystification
behind the noble declarations of principle about freedom and cooperation among peoples. Austen Chamberlain begged him to continue his help "until the situation is more clearly defined."[7]

On 26 May Keynes replied:

> I appreciate your letter very much, just as I have had good reason to
> appreciate my treatment by the Treasury all through; and if my only
> grounds for leaving were the need of a rest and the desire to get
> back to my own work, I could not resist your appeal. But that is not
> the position. . . . We have presented a draft treaty to the Germans
> which contains in it much that is unjust and much more that is inex-
> pedient. Until the last moment no one could appreciate its full bear-
> ing. It is now right and necessary to discuss it with the Germans and
> to be ready to make substantial concessions. If this policy is not pur-
> sued, the consequences will be disastrous in the extreme.
>
> If, therefore, the decision is taken to discuss the treaty with
> the Germans with a view to substantial changes and if our policy is
> such that it looks as if I can be of real use, I am ready to stay another
> two or three weeks. But if the decision is otherwise, I fear that I
> must resign immediately. I cannot express how strongly I feel as to
> the gravity of what is in front of us, and I must have my hands quite
> free. I wish I could talk to you about the whole miserable business.

---

5. *C.W.K.* 16:440–41.
6. Ibid., p. 441. (In all quotations the italics duplicate the original.)
7. Ibid., p. 459.

The Prime Minister is leading us all into a morass of destruction. The settlement which he is proposing for Europe disrupts it economically and must depopulate it by millions of persons.[8]

On 5 June he officially informed Lloyd George of his resignation. Shortly afterward he left Paris.

Quite apart from political dissent, what were the deeper, underlying reasons that led the well-balanced, rational Keynes to make a tempestuous gesture in such a delicate moment for the future of Britain and Europe? Keynes gave these reasons in *The Economic Consequences of the Peace*, which was written in just a few months and published at the end of 1919. He had resigned to free his hands. He wanted to be able to cry out loud that the treaty contained clauses that were "inexpedient and unjust." He wanted to shake public opinion in the hope of forcing the politicians in the guise of statesmen to reveal their true aims. The British electorate had to be made aware that Lloyd George had exploited war reparations to galvanize his own campaign for the 1918 General Elections, and that the revanchist stance toward Germany was better adapted to winning votes for the government coalition than to promoting the well-being of Great Britain and Europe. Above all, voters had to be apprised of the economic realities in Europe and the dire consequences if the treaty were implemented.

Keynes insisted that Germany had been a major catalyst in the rapid European economic growth from 1870 to the outbreak of war. The main features of German economic growth paralleled those that had characterized the development of the rest of the old continent: increased productivity, intensified international trade, and access to the fertile soils and the agricultural products of America, Africa, and Asia. Even prior to the war the tranquillity of the process had been shaken by some basic fragility.

It would have been very difficult for this system to survive in the face of any external disruptions; now it had to deal with a cataclysm that had torn its roots:

The war had so shaken this system as to endanger the life of Europe altogether. A great part of the continent was sick and dying; its pop-

8. Ibid., pp. 459–60.

ulation was greatly in excess of the numbers for which a livelihood was available; its organisation was destroyed, its transport system ruptured, and its food supplies terribly impaired.

It was the task of the peace conference to honour engagements and to satisfy justice; but no less to re-establish life and to heal wounds. These tasks were dictated as much by prudence as by the magnanimity which the wisdom of antiquity approved in victors.[9]

The Council of Four, however, had other objectives to plague them. Once Clemenceau's "Carthiginian Peace" had overshadowed Wilson's lofty Fourteen Points, the Council took aim at the systematic demolition of the German economic system. The treaty forced Germany to accept: (1) an almost complete cession of her merchant fleet; (2) the cession to the Allies of all her overseas possessions; (3) the reannexation by France of Alsace and Lorraine, and the confiscation of German property in these regions; (4) the cession to France of the Saar coal basin and the obligation for a number of years to supply France, Belgium, Italy, and Luxembourg with an annual average of about 40 million tons of coal; (5) the cession of Silesia to Poland, unless a plebiscite decided otherwise; (6) customs tariffs that gave the Allies most-favored-nation treatment without reciprocity; and (7) the cession of rolling stock and the granting of improved tariff rates for Allied goods transported by rail to Germany.

Undoubtedly these clauses in the treaty sought to destroy the foundations on which German development rested—internationally in her relations with her colonies, and domestically in her exemplary coal and steel industry.

Keynes pointed out that 75 percent of German iron ore originated in Alsace and Lorraine. At the same time the onerous clauses on coal implied an absurd German commitment to supply 40 million tons out of a total annual production that had fallen to 100 million—despite the fact that her domestic demand alone amounted, at a conservative estimate, to 110 million. Keynes warned:

But it is evident that Germany cannot and will not furnish the Allies with a contribution of 40 million tons annually. Those Allied ministers who have told their peoples that she can have certainly deceived them for the sake of allaying for the moment the misgivings of the

9. *Economic Consequences*, in *C.W.K.* 2:15–16.

European peoples as to the path along which they are being led. The presence of these illusory provisions (amongst others) in the clauses of the treaty of peace is especially charged with danger for the future. . . .

If the distribution of the European coal supplies is to be a scramble in which France is satisfied first, Italy next, and everyone else takes their chance, the industrial future of Europe is black and the prospects of revolution very good.[10]

In addition to these obligations Germany had to pay war reparations. The commitment, entered into at the time of the armistice, derived from a clause in Wilson's Fourteen Points according to which Germany had to give "compensation for all damage done to civilians and their property by land, by sea, and from the air."

The clause was vaguely formulated and allowed a wide degree of latitude on the interpretation of "damage." It was ridiculous, however, to see it as an obligation for Germany to reimburse the "full" cost of the war, but this did not prevent France from adopting precisely this extravagant interpretation; Britain, for her part, was constrained by the line taken by Lloyd George during the election campaign, committing Germany to pay all the war damages up to the limits of her capacity.

Thus the treaty provided for reparations not only for damages to civilian life and property, but also for all war-linked domestic subsidies and pensions granted by the Allied countries. Keynes calculated that this was equivalent to imposing a financial burden on Germany of some £8,000 million. Even assuming that the Germans were able to begin repayment of principal and interest immediately, the treaty clauses implied that each annual payment installment would amount to £480 million, a forbidding sum. Keynes estimated that by the end of 1921 the Germans would be able to realize between £250 and £350 million, through the sale of gold, ships, foreign assets, and rolling stock. Analyzing imports and exports, item by item, he calculated a maximum possible balance of payments surplus of £100 million. Allowing 5 percent for interest, and 1 percent for repayment of capital, over a period of thirty years, this represented a capital sum having a present value of £1,700 million. The maximum sum with which Germany might be burdened could not therefore exceed £2,000 million.

---

10. Ibid., pp. 58–60.

The attempt to load Germany with the whole burden of European reconstruction was politically short-sighted and economically nonviable. The political short-sightedness consisted in the failure to realize that the imposition of an impossible burden on Germany would shatter the existing social order and hasten the seizure of power by demagogic extremist forces. This would stir a European political crisis which would inevitably be inimical to democracy: there was the Russian example already at hand.[11]

The economic blunder, on the other hand, lay in the fact that it was objectively impossible for the German economy to free enough real resources to fulfill Germany's treaty obligations. Living standards could not be reduced below a subsistence level: furthermore, if Germany was ever to be able to honor the treaty terms a considerable proportion of her available resources would have to be devoted first to her own domestic reconstruction. Even if one assumed that Germany could achieve sufficient exports to create a balance of payments surplus compatible with the reparations being contemplated, results could be devastating for the Allies' foreign trade. The previous fifty years provided an object lesson in showing that countries do not develop in isolation from one another. Europe's prospects were, moreover, not favorable. Her productive capacity had fallen; the transport system had disintegrated; everyone was meeting hardships in acquiring supplies from the traditional overseas markets.

It was in the interest of the future of Europe that the treaty be radically revised. Any revision would have to include: (1) the reduction of the total reparations to £1,500 million, payable in thirty interest-free installments, beginning in 1923; (2) the complete cancellation of all inter-Allied debts; and (3) issuance of an international loan to all belligerents, underwritten to a large extent by the United States, and to be drawn on for the purchase of food and raw materials.

Does the position taken by Keynes, and his experience as an economist thrown into a den of politicians, permit us to glean anything further in our attempt to reconstruct his own educational quest

---

11. On this point see V. H. Fleisig, "War-related Debts and the Great Depression," *American Economic Review*, Papers and Proceedings, May 1976.

on the nature of capitalism? His life in this period was marked by the huge scale of the human drama witnessed firsthand with a keen and conscious sense of responsibility for decisions that would affect the fate of hundreds of millions of people. A reflective evaluation of the options and the wisdom of the decisions required a profound analysis, and above all, an intuitive historical sense in ordering the forces responsible for the development of Western civilization and for its stability and viability over time, and an understanding of the conditions necessary to maintain the social balance. The only way in which the treaty could be judged seriously was on the basis of a clear vision of complex and fundamental questions. On this occasion, as in his youthful past, Keynes never sought refuge in vagueness.

He states, at the beginning of the *Economic Consequences of the Peace*, that the economic development of the Western world had depended on the organization of European societies and economies in such a way as to maximize the accumulation of capital. The two factors mostly responsible for the vast accumulation over the previous fifty years had been (1) an unequal distribution of income in favor of the capitalist class and (2) the implied acquiescence by that class in a low propensity to consume. These conditions, on their own, would have been insufficient to fuel the process had it not been for the unspoken social consensus, or what Keynes called "the psychology of society." He surmised that the basic philosophy that had permeated Western society and fostered its stable and coherent development could be summed up as follows:

> Thus this remarkable system depended for its growth on a double bluff or deception. On the one hand the labouring classes accepted from ignorance or powerlessness, or were compelled, persuaded, or cajoled by custom, convention, authority, and the well-established order of society into accepting, a situation in which they could call their own very little of the cake that they and nature and the capitalists were co-operating to produce. And on the other hand the capitalist classes were allowed to call the best part of the cake theirs and were theoretically free to consume it, on the tacit underlying condition that they consumed very little of it in practice. The duty of "saving" became nine-tenths of virtue and the growth of the cake the object of true religion. There grew round the non-consumption of the cake all those instincts of puritanism which in other ages has withdrawn itself from the world and has neglected

the arts of production as well as those of enjoyment. And so the cake increased; but to what end was not clearly contemplated. Individuals would be exhorted not so much to abstain as to defer, and to culti-vate the pleasures of security and anticipation. Saving was for old age or for your child; but this was only in theory—the virtue of the cake was that it was never to be consumed, neither by you nor by your children after you. (Pp. 11–12)

This "double bluff" did not lie however in the unequal distri-bution of income, considered in its own right, but rather in the risk that the rules of the game might fall apart before the expected, beneficial results were achieved. If the cake had been able to grow at an adequate rate vis-à-vis the growth of the population, the sac-rifices made would have been repaid, and economics would have ceased to be the "dismal science" of the classical economists. There was, however, not the least reason to expect that the population would grow in some special proportion to capital accumulation; nor—and this was even more important—could it be hoped to achieve a stable consensus in favor of an unequal distribution of income:

> In writing thus I do not necessarily disparage the practices of that generation. In the unconscious recesses of its being society knew what it was about . . . I seek only to point out that the principle of accumulation based on inequality was a vital part of the pre-war or-der of society and of progress as we then understood it, and to em-phasise that this principle depended on unstable psychological conditions, which it may be impossible to re-create. It was not nat-ural for a population, of whom so few enjoyed the comforts of life, to accumulate so hugely. The war has disclosed the possibility of con-sumption to all and the vanity of abstinence to many. Thus the bluff is discovered; the labouring classes may be no longer willing to forgo so largely, and the capitalist classes may be no longer confident of the future, may seek to enjoy more fully their liberties of consump-tion so long as they last, and thus precipitate the hour of their con-fiscation. (Pp. 12–13)

Even if it were granted that the European countries might have continued to amass and accumulate for some time longer, an-other factor of instability was already at work, even before 1914. This consisted of the revised relationship between the capitalist countries of the old and the new worlds. The strong increase in the population of the Americas had decreased the agricultural surplus available for export, and increased its price. As a result, the previously favorable terms of trade between European industrial goods and American agricultural produce had deteriorated. Further, the explosive development of U.S. industry had made European industrial produce ever less appealing, making it harder, and more urgent, for Europe to find alternative outlets for its customary export wares. What Keynes seemed to be grasping, and conveying, was that in the European system after 1870, where international exchange was based primarily on the export of goods and capital from industrial to developing areas of the globe, foreign trade was a very precarious foundation on which to base the stability of the generalized development process.

The war had caused these elements of instability in the system to erode, seriously weakening the foundations for a recovery. At the same time, particularly in Germany, the countries of the Austro-Hungarian empire, and Italy, hyperinflation had raised its ugly head. For five years the war had absorbed an overwhelming proportion of Europe's real resources; inflation seemed nothing more than a natural and inevitable consequence of the impossibility of crushing consumption to the same extent as the fall in productive capacity. The cancellation of inter-Allied debts, and the availability of the American loan, were the only ways of halting the price increases and stimulating a growth recovery. It was senseless, however, to hope that it might be possible to squeeze an unlimited volume of resources from Germany without accelerating German inflation. To Keynes, inflation was capable of sapping the very foundations of capitalist society, and the social order on which it was built:

Lenin is said to have declared that the best way to destroy the capitalist system was to debauch the currency. By a continuing process of inflation, governments can confiscate, secretly and unobserved, an important part of the wealth of their citizens. By this method they not only confiscate, but they confiscate *arbitrarily*; and, while the process impoverishes many, it actually enriches some. The sight of this arbitrary rearrangement of riches strikes not only at security, but at confidence in the equity of the existing distribution of wealth. . . . As the inflation proceeds and the real value of the currency fluctuates wildly from month to month, all permanent relations between debtors and creditors, which form the ultimate foundation of capitalism, become so utterly disordered as to be almost meaningless; and the process of wealth-getting degenerates into a gamble and a lottery. (Pp. 148–49)

In this "gamble" it was the most enterprising among the capitalists who managed to profit from the situation, transforming themselves, at times independently of any particular will to do so, into "profiteers." As a result they attracted not only the hatred of the proletariat but even that of the bourgeoisie. Inflation-prone governments thus bore responsibility for the crisis engendered within the "entrepreneur class"; they were undermining the credibility of the system without having "any program to put in its place." In addition to the social and economic disorder caused by the disruption of contractual relationships, inflation inflicted a state of insecurity and timidity on the entrepreneur class, inhibiting it from performing the role in accumulation that it had played over the previous half century:

> We are thus faced in Europe with the spectacle of an extraordinary weakness on the part of the great capitalist class, which has emerged from the industrial triumphs of the nineteenth century, and seemed a very few years ago our all-powerful master. The terror and personal timidity of the individuals of this class is now so great, their confidence in their place in society and in their necessity to the social organism so diminished, that they are the easy victims of intimidation. . . . Now they tremble before every insult—call them pro-Germans, international financiers, or profiteers, and they will give you any ransom you choose to ask not to speak of them so harshly. They allow themselves to be ruined and altogether undone by their own instruments, governments of their own making, and a Press of which they are the proprietors. Perhaps it is historically true that no order of society ever perishes save by its own hand. In the complexer world of Western Europe the Immanent Will may achieve its ends more subtly and bring in the revolution no less inevitably through a Klotz or a George than by the intellectualisms, too ruthless and self-conscious for us, of the bloodthirsty philosophers of Russia. (P. 150)

Keynes was thus explicit and alarmed over the effects of inflation on the capitalist system. Inflation, however, never seemed to be a necessary consequence of capitalist development. Rather, it was a result of an onerous war, or a shock exogenous to the normal system. He was reticent, compared to Marxist critics, on the "inevitability" of war in the capitalist context. The fact remained, however, that capitalism was not just vulnerable to an exogenous inflation; instability was fed by the very working of the system.

Given his analysis, what was Keynes's normative attitude? Was the private system of accumulation still valid when once corrected by adequate outside intervention? Or was it in need of some radical surgery? What prompted Keynes's frequent allusions to the Russian "bolshevik" system, recently installed?

To a modern reader of *The Economic Consequences of the Peace* with some knowledge of Keynes's subsequent work, these questions are tantalizing. Obviously, the post-World War II era imparts an experience with a period of capitalism which Keynes never knew: a simple judgment could not even be elicited from looking at the totality of his writings. Nonetheless, if we consider Keynes's opinions on European development, together with certain of his reflections on the Soviet system published a few years later, we find some clues to interpret his conception of capitalism in the period around the 1920s.

In September 1925, immediately following his marriage to the ballerina Lydia Lopokova, Keynes visited Russia for the celebration of the second centenary of the Academy of the Sciences, where he represented Cambridge University. On his return he gave his impressions in three articles published in the *Nation and Athenaeum* and later reprinted as *A Short View of Russia.*[12] The general content of the articles discloses a sincere attempt at a calm evaluation of a country with which he had been unable to acquaint himself in depth, and of a socioeconomic system which prejudice had surrounded with a "belt of mist."

Keynes risked a number of positive comments on the improved living standards achieved by the Soviet economy since the war, and on the progress made toward completing some of the new regime's major projects. At the same time he severely criticized the policy whereby the fixing of a system of relative prices, extremely unfavorable to agriculture, was used to transfer income to workers in industry. This policy was made possible by the state monopoly on imports and exports. On the one hand, the breaking of the link between domestic and international prices enabled the regime to compensate for the inefficiencies of the industrial system, and to

---

12. Reprinted in *C.W.K.* 9.

protect the external value of the ruble; on the other, it discouraged agricultural production, which in Keynes's view represented the "real wealth of the nation," and attracted a growing number of peasants to the cities, the only effect being to augment unemployment.

These critical observations were not, however, at the center of Keynes's deeper concerns, which concentrated on the nature of the new social order that the October revolution had established in Russia. For Keynes, the essential connotation of Leninism was its injection of a new religion involving a "sublimation of materialist egotism" through absorption in an "ineffable mystic union" or "in the pursuit of an ideal of life for the whole of society." To avoid being misunderstood in his use of this term, he gave a number of concrete examples of what he meant:

> Some instances from our latter-day celebrities may illustrate my explanation. Certain of the politicians of France, M. Poincaré for example, followed hard by some of the politicians of the United States, seem to me to be amongst the most irreligious men now in the world; Trotsky, Mr Bernard Shaw, and Mr Baldwin, each in his way, amongst the most religious. (P. 254)

Leninism has all the connotations of other new religions: it "derives its power from a small minority of enthusiastic converts"; "it seems to take the colour and gaiety and freedom out of everyday life"; "it persecutes without justice or pity those who actively resist it"; and "it is filled with missionary ardour and œcumenical ambitions" (pp. 256–57).

But was it a religion capable of attracting modern man? This was the ultimate question with which Keynes was wrestling. He was extremely sure of himself in his declaration that he was "not ready for a creed which does not care how much it destroys the liberty and security of daily life, which uses deliberately the weapons of persecution, destruction, and international strife" (p. 258).

He admitted, however, that to limit oneself to these aspects would be to lose the essence of the new religion; communists had always declared that they belonged to a transitory, revolutionary phase and that they had no place in its final stage of development. What, he asked, was the essence of communism as a new social order?

In one respect Communism but follows other famous religions. It exalts the common man and makes him everything. Here there is nothing new. But there is another factor in it which also is not new but which may, nevertheless, in a changed form and a new setting, contribute something to the true religion of the future, if there be any true religion. *Leninism is absolutely non-supernatural, and its emotional and ethical essence centres about the individual's and the community's attitude towards the love of money.* (P. 259)

Keynes believed, in other words, that the key characteristic around which Russian communism was attempting to structure a new society was a new attitude toward the pursuit of profit, what he summed up as "the love of money." The system was moving in this direction not so much by prohibiting those activities which in the West were typically motivated by profit but rather by making them "precarious and dishonorable":

> Even the most admirable aspects of the love of money in our existing society, such as thrift and saving, and the attainment of financial security and independence for one's self and one's family, whilst not deemed morally wrong, will be rendered so difficult and impracticable as to be not worth while. Everyone should work for the community—the new creed runs—and, if he does his duty, the community will uphold him. (P. 260)

Such a change in attitude toward profit and money was extremely significant for the future of a society. It could be that it was utopian. Was it really possible, however, to say, as many did, that it was "insincere or perverse"? This, Keynes claimed, was the real ground on which communism's prospects should be judged. As far as its contribution to solving economic problems was concerned, it had nothing to offer which could not be applied, equally or more successfully, in bourgeois societies. As a religion—a force capable of amalgamating the different components of society by showing them a future to which to commit themselves—communism had a good chance of prevailing over capitalism. Capitalism, after all, was "absolutely irreligious, without internal union, without much public spirit, often, though not always, a mere congeries of possessors and pursuers" (p. 267).

Its economic efficiency might not be enough to compensate a communist society's faith in the future. Now that the doubt had

wormed itself into capitalism that maybe a better future would never arrive, it would have to be many times more efficient than communism if it were to beat off the challenge.

It seems to me that the substance of these reflections on Russia shows at least a degree of continuity with Keynes's observations of 1919 on the development of European capitalism. To begin with, he restates—this time more explicitly—his aversion for the anti-democratic methods used by Leninism to impose the new creed on Russian society. At the same time, however, he is prepared to admit that these belong to the revolutionary or transitional stage of communism. As far as the final stage is concerned—the new social order that communism aims to establish—Keynes rejects its economic aspects; he does not believe that revolution is ever necessary to achieve these. He does reveal, however, a sympathy for the new moral climate that is supposed to mark economic relations in a communist society, where Leninism seeks "a combination of two things which Europeans have kept for some centuries in different compartments of the soul—religion and business" (p. 256).

The main factor of instability in capitalism, according to Keynes in *The Economic Consequences of the Peace*, is precisely the fragility of the social relations underlying the accumulation process; implicitly, he leans toward the view that capitalism could be made less unstable by modifying the basic moral motivations behind economic activity. Keynes's thought processes are far removed from Marx's analytical methods, where a change in social relations is inconceivable without a change in production relations. It is far-fetched, therefore, to imagine elements of Marxism in Keynes's thinking.[13] For our study we need only bear in mind the terms in which, by the mid 1920s, Keynes had posed the vexatious problems that troubled his mind. This will help in understanding his later intellectual resolution of the key issues.

---

13. We have no information to the effect that Keynes ever made a serious study of Marx's thought.

CHAPTER 3

INFLATION, DEFLATION, AND THE RETURN TO GOLD

During the 1920s the economic performance of the Western world, especially of Great Britain, offered Keynes new opportunities to reflect on the perplexities of the capitalist system. The war and the peace talks had led him to consider the latent causes of instability in the process of capital accumulation; he had prophesied the enormous dangers to freedom and the menace to the democratic social order that would ensue from impossible exactions on the defeated powers. Now, European reconstruction and obstinate policies aimed at restoring prewar monetary mechanisms brought him face to face with a new and virulent form of instability: inflation (or, antithetically, deflation) and unemployment.

Keynes's early warnings against inflation appeared in *The Economic Consequences of the Peace*. If European reconstruction were based on pointless inter-Allied squabbling over looting the losers' remaining riches, instead of fostering a recovery of production, he believed inflation was inevitable. Within two years the prophecy was tragically confirmed by German and Austrian hyperinflation. The smashing of these countries' monetary institutions prepared the groundwork for the democratic crisis in which the advent of unemployment provided a fertile audience for Naziism. In Russia, too, the period between 1920 and 1923 was marked by a dizzy price explosion which made the ruble about as valuable as printed paper.

Between the summer of 1919 and the autumn of 1920, Britain and the United States both experienced rising prices—in Britain the increase was somewhat higher. There followed a period of deflation which lasted until autumn 1922.

The violent fluctuations in the purchasing power of money thus appeared as a concrete threat to any resumption of growth in an atmosphere of stability. Instead of being an exceptional and occasional occurrence tied to unusual events such as a great war, inflation risked becoming a way of life, a sacrifice on the altar of reconstruction. In many quarters even broaching the idea that the authorities should exert some kind of control over the sequence of expansion and recession was looked on with grave misgivings. In Great Britain, large sectors of public opinion, as well as the Treasury and the central bank, tended to see government wartime manipulation and intervention in the economy as the actual cause of the price disorder. The corollary to this interpretation was the opinion that the only good solution was a return to the "rules of the game," meaning mechanisms capable of automatically regulating the monetary system. For almost a century the gold standard had been an article of faith. What then was the cost of a return to gold? Was it a simple nostalgic yearning for the past stemming from barely concealed vested interests, or did it rest on solid economic rationality?

These were the options of "informed" debate in Britain in 1922. Analysis of reality merged with value judgments, with class interest conflicting with righteous statements of moral principle and each side sustaining its propositions by a selective use of economic theory.

Keynes had published a brief book in January 1922, *The Revision of the Treaty*.[1] Now that his mission to mold and inform public opinion about the peace treaty was over, and as the force of events was pushing to validate the results he had foreseen, he published a series of articles in the Reconstruction Supplements of the *Manchester Guardian Commercial*.[2] A year later he used part of the same material for a more rigorous analysis of the effects of inflation and deflation, at home and in foreign relations, and of the monetary policy options available to achieve the alternative goals of price or exchange-rate stability.

In *A Tract on Monetary Reform* Keynes once again attacked a burning public issue of his time.[3] He clarified the terms of the

---

1. (London: Macmillan); reprinted in *C.W.K.*, vol. 3.
2. "The Theory of the Exchanges and Purchasing Power Parity," 20 April 1922; "The Forward Market in Foreign Exchange," 20 April 1922; "Inflation as a Method of Taxation," 27 July 1922; and "The Consequence to Society of Changes in the Value of Money," 27 July 1922.
3. (London: Macmillan, 1923); reprinted in *C.W.K.*, vol. 4.

question, considered their implications, and drew the logical consequences for economic policy. He described the dangers inherent in drift, anticipating with his uncanny gift for economic prophecy the future course of development and dispelling much of the confusion that was rampant.

The following passage from the preface to his book provides an enlightening answer about the stage to which his thought had progressed in his search for the nerve center of the capitalist system:

> We leave saving to the private investor, and we encourage him to place his savings mainly in titles to money. We leave the responsibility for setting production in motion to the business man, who is mainly influenced by the profits which he expects to accrue to himself in terms of money. Those who are not in favour of drastic changes in the existing organisation of society believe that these arrangements, being in accord with human nature, have great advantages. But they cannot work properly if the money, which they assume as a stable measuring-rod, is undependable. Unemployment, the precarious life of the worker, the disappointment of expectation, the sudden loss of savings, the excessive windfalls to individuals, the speculator, the profiteer—all proceed, in large measure, from the instability of the standard of value.

Keynes thus identified the erosion of the purchasing power of money as a vital crisis organ capable of rupture in the capitalist accumulation mechanism: the instability of money was itself a signal of the crisis in the system. He was not yet ready, however, to analyze the endogenous forces underlying the instability, which he tended to attribute to forces external to the economic system. He thus concentrated on the channels through which inflation and deflation exert their deleterious effects on "decisions to save and to invest," and hence on employment and growth. This was the first time that he isolated and subjected to rigorous analysis some of those elements of instability in the "psychology of society" mentioned in *The Economic Consequences of the Peace* as responsible for the fragility of the capitalist mode of accumulation.

Why should there be concern about variations in the general level of prices if these were adequately compensated by upswings in money income? The level of employment in a given economic system is determined, it was then thought, simultaneously with the real "equilibrium" wage that results from the balancing of demand and supply on the labor market. If prices and earnings vary proportionately, real wages remain constant. Unemployment is a unique concern only to workers who are unwilling to accept the "equilibrium" wage. Variations in the quantity of money in circulation alone affect the price level. Nominal values move up and down with the money supply; relative prices are unchanged. So long as the external value of the currency, as expressed by the exchange rate, rises or falls adequately, there is no reason for the real magnitudes within the system to change.

This, roughly speaking, was the dominant theoretical notion at Cambridge in the early 1920s. It rested on the quantity theory of money which Marshall had elaborated and which Keynes himself taught for many years. Later Keynes was to launch a frontal attack on the futility of the mechanism for perfectly balancing investment and savings.

In 1923 Keynes had merely limited himself to rejecting a corollary of the theory, namely, that variations in the value of money were neutral vis-à-vis real magnitudes in the economic system. This was not as yet a repudiation of the whole theoretical paradigm inherited from the old "masters" and still professed by eminent colleagues such as Arthur C. Pigou, Ralph G. Hawtrey, and Dennis H. Robertson. What Keynes did contest was the total lack of realism in the dominant theory with regard to the speed and flexibility with which prices and wages in the different sectors, and the monetary incomes of the different social classes, would have to adjust if variations in the purchasing power of money were not to disrupt savings, investment, employment, and output.

Keynes's fundamental observation was that inflation and deflation modify the distribution of wealth among the social classes, and thus the production and accumulation of new wealth. Capitalist accumulation is based on an institutional system in which those who receive incomes are divided into fairly distinct social classes. Owing to the differing nature of their incomes, and of their respective roles in production, each is affected differently by movements in the general level of prices. Keynes distinguishes between savers, whose income is primarily derived from investment in bonds with a fixed monetary return, entrepreneurs (or "businessmen"), and wage-earners.

These distinctions were suggested by the actual history of the development process during the nineteenth century. The separation between the ownership and the control of wealth had come about in various ways. Keynes observed that the most highly developed of these had been the lending of sums of money at a predetermined rate of interest. The lenders had been the propertied and professional classes; the borrowers the entrepreneurs. This system of accumulation had been favored by a long period of basically stable prices, almost from the end of the Napoleonic wars right up to World War I. Given the tendency of prices to remain stable, or even to fall during the last quarter of the nineteenth century, owners of wealth who had put their money out on hire conserved or augmented their fortunes. They were thus encouraged to further accumulation and, in this way, supplied the entrepreneurs with the financial wherewithal to achieve an accumulation of real capital. Thus the stability in the purchasing power of money facilitated the long era of growth:

> For a hundred years the system worked, throughout Europe, with an extraordinary success and facilitated the growth of wealth on an unprecedented scale. To save and to invest became at once the duty and the delight of a large class. The savings were seldom drawn on, and, accumulating at compound interest, made possible the material triumphs which we now all take for granted. The morals, the politics, the literature, and the religion of the age joined in a grand conspiracy for the promotion of saving. God and Mammon were reconciled. Peace on earth to men of good means. A rich man could, after all, enter into the Kingdom of Heaven—if only he saved. (P. 6)

There was, however, no rational or imperative reason to expect the purchasing power of money to remain stable. A long view of history yields the opposite impression, namely, that price fluctuations are the rule and the experience of the nineteenth century an exception. There existed two forces in particular which might logically have been expected to push up prices. One of these was the state, the other the entrepreneurs; both might gain from an inflation that reduced their debt burden. In Keynes's words, "this progressive deterioration in the value of money through history is not an accident, and has behind it two great driving forces—the impecuniosity of governments and the superior political influence of the debtor class" (p. 8).

In any case, regardless of what might or might not be expected on logical grounds, the fact was that in the space of just a few years, between 1914 and 1920, the purchasing power of the bills that made up the British consolidated debt had fallen by one-third, and that of their income by two-thirds. In other words, "the pre-war savings of the middle class, so far as they were invested in bonds, mortgages, or bank deposits, have been largely or entirely wiped out" (p. 16).

All this was bound to discourage saving. It implied a turn-about in the "social psychology" that had been the engine of the last three generations' capital accumulation.

Given the way in which it was structured, however, the system could not afford to halt the growth in the stock of capital: its population was continually climbing; an insufficient expansion of the capital means of production would make it impossible to main-tain, much less to raise living standards.

While inflation hurt the rentier, it benefited the entrepreneur and the businessman, for two basic reasons. First, one had to con-sider the way in which the entrepreneurial class was favored by the real diminution of its past debts; second, inflation provided an in-strument for speculative profits. Anyone who had bought goods, or factors of production, at one price and later sold them at a higher one profited. The expectation of further price escalation encour-aged production and capital stock-building (as in inventory). In these conditions industry and trade became a gamble which one could only win as long as prices moved upward. Businessmen became uninhibited about indebting themselves at ever higher nominal in-terest rates, encouraged by the fact that the expected price in-creases were always below those that actually occurred so that the real rate of interest they were paying was falling. Speculative prof-its, however, were a double-edged weapon: they benefited in-dividual entrepreneurs, but the entire entrepreneurial class was discredited in the eyes of society. The infamy that covered the busi-ness community distorted the very nature of entrepreneurial activ-ity and its functioning in the accumulation process:

> To the consumer the business man's exceptional profits appear as the cause (instead of the consequence) of the hated rise of prices. Amidst the rapid fluctuations of his fortunes he himself loses his conserva-tive instincts, and begins to think more of the large gains of the moment than of the lesser, but permanent, profits of normal busi-

ness. The welfare of his enterprise in the relatively distant future weighs less with him than before, and thoughts are excited of a quick fortune and clearing out. His excessive gains have come to him unsought and without fault or design on his part, but once acquired he does not lightly surrender them, and will struggle to retain his booty. . . . No man of spirit will consent to remain poor if he believes his betters to have gained their goods by lucky gambling. To convert the business man into the profiteer is to strike a blow at capitalism, because it destroys the psychological equilibrium which permits the perpetuance of unequal rewards. The economic doctrine of normal profits, vaguely apprehended by everyone, is a necessary condition for the justification of capitalism. (Pp. 23–24)

If, as had always occurred in the past, wages failed to keep pace with prices,[4] the wage-earning class was burdened by inflation. Keynes observed, however, that in the inflationary postwar atmosphere a number of well-organized groups of unionized workers had succeeded not only in winning reductions in working hours but also in gaining pay rises equivalent to, and at times higher than, the rate of inflation. These fortunate workers had achieved an improvement in their relative position at a time when the overall wealth of society had fallen. Nonetheless, their organizational strength would not have been enough to succeed had the entrepreneurs' speculative super-profits not led them to take a softer line on wage demands. The improvement wage earners had achieved was socially desirable but not necessarily stable. If the new structure of income distribution did not correspond to "a permanent modification of the economic factors which determine the distribution of national product between different classes," but was just "due to some temporary and exhaustible influence connected with inflation and with the resulting disturbance in the standard of value," it would be a flimsy one-time thing.[5] For a while, high inflation could conceal the squandering of society's accumulated wealth simply by weakening the distinction between income and capital: society could decumulate real capital and distribute it as income, hiding the fact in the impressive purely nominal appreciation of fixed capital.

4. See on this point, P. Ciocca, "L'ipotesi del ritardo dei salari rispetto ai prezzi in periodi di inflazione: Alcune considerazioni generali," *Bancaria*, May 1969, and his valuable extensive bibliography.

5. *Tract on Monetary Reform*, in *C.W.K.* 4:27.

Given the manifold ways in which inflation redistributed wealth and the fragile nexus of the social and institutional structure of capitalism, it was inconceivable that inflation would not have a profound effect on production and accumulation. An opposite trend in prices—deflation and deflationary expectations—would exert what could well be an even more debilitating influence on activity. Modern techniques of production lengthen the period between the hire of factors of production and the sale of the finished product. Despite technical progress in transportation, domestic and international trade over greater distances extends the time that has to elapse between production and consumption so that, in a nonbarter economy, it increases the risk for the entrepreneur: he might not realize a sufficiently high margin to cover his costs and guarantee a residual profit. The danger was not so much in a change of relative prices—this could not be avoided even in a barter economy. The real peril would come from a fall in the general level of prices:

> But there is also a considerable risk directly arising out of instability in the value of money. During the lengthy process of production the business world is incurring outgoings in terms of *money*—paying out in money for wages and other expenses of production—in the expectation of recouping this outlay by disposing of the product for *money* at a later date. That is to say, the business world as a whole must always be in a position where it stands to gain by a rise of price and to lose by a fall of price. Whether he likes it or not, the technique of production under a régime of money contract forces the business world always to carry a big speculative position; and if it is reluctant to carry this position, the productive process must be slackened. (P. 33)

The natural consequence of this paralysis of production would be unemployment and, in a cumulative process, this would sponsor expectations of further price reductions and thus a secondary drop in production. At the same time the increase in debt burden would make the entrepreneurs' financial position precarious. For the state, the public debt would become unbearable. Implied would be a massive transfer of wealth to rentiers.[6] Economic initiative and

---

6. The deflationary effects of an increase in the real value of debts owes a great deal to the brilliant interpretation of the Great Depression by Irving Fisher, "The Debt-Deflation Theory of Great Depressions," *Econometrica* (1933), pp. 337–57.

the government's ability to spend would be seriously depressed and hinder subsequent recovery.

Excluding the savage inflation on German lines, Keynes believed that if one had to choose between inflation and deflation, the former might well be the lesser evil. The real objective, however, was to eliminate both evils. The first step had to be to radically change politicians' perceptions and those of the public who imagined that the value of money was entirely determined by the play of economic forces within the system and was therefore immune to any form of control:

> We must free ourselves from the deep distrust which exists against allowing the regulation of the standard of value to be the subject of *deliberate decision*. We can no longer afford to leave it in the category of which the distinguishing characteristics are possessed in different degrees by the weather, the birth rate, and the Constitution—matters which are settled by natural causes, or are the resultant of the separate action of many individuals acting independently, or require a revolution to change them.[7]

The idea that the value of money depends on the spontaneous workings of the system descended from a whole tradition in economic thought. The prevalent Cambridge doctrine was inherited from Marshall and abetted by Pigou's contributions. Keynes's *A Tract on Monetary Reform* adhered to the orthodoxy though he did argue the need not to leave the value of money to lean with the wind. Nonetheless, his interpretation of the quantity theory of money, in inflation and deflation, and his evaluation of the overall effects of policy on money and credit laid the grounds for his subsequent important theoretical reversal which constituted his original lasting contribution to the analysis of capitalism.

In line with the Cambridge doctrine Keynes saw the quantity theory of money as a theoretical proposition whose "correspondence with fact is not open to question" (p. 61).

It is a fact, in other words, that people hold a part of their wealth in money and that the amount of money they hold depends on the purchasing power they think it wise to hold in liquid form. The amount of purchasing power people want to have on hand is determined by their wealth and habits. Habits in the use of money

---

7. *Tract on Monetary Reform*, in *C.W.K.* 4:36.

depend on how often the user is paid, on how often he pays suppliers, and on the frequency of his use of bank money and his desire to hoard. Therefore, if, in Keynes's symbols, n is the quantity of money, k the quantity of goods the holders of money wish to be able to buy, and p the price level of these goods, we are inevitably led to the truistic relation $n = pk$.

This equation, Keynes observed, has often been interpreted as expressing a proportional relationship between n and p. The quantity theory of money has been interpreted to mean that doubling the quantity of money would double the price level. Implied is that k is constant. Now it may be reasonable to argue that in the long term, once all the effects of the variation in the quantity of money have been absorbed, k may return to a "normal" value. Far less acceptable is the hypothesis that while the quantity of money changes k does not. What is really relevant is the way economic phenomena behave in the conjunction of events; statements about the long-term result are not particularly enlightening: "*In the long run* we are all dead. Economists set themselves too easy, too useless a task if in tempestuous seasons they can only tell us that when the storm is long past the ocean is flat again" (p. 65).

According to Keynes, practical experience clearly shows that variations in the quantity of money lead to changes in monetary habits and thus to variations in k. In the past, during the early phases of an inflationary process, people have had the impression that they were richer than before and have sought to hold more purchasing power in liquid form. The result has been that prices have risen less than the quantity of money. On the other hand, during the more advanced stages of inflation, when widespread expectations have been formed of further spiraling, there has usually been an opposite reaction: the public has acted to reduce its money stocks, rapidly ridding itself of cash which depreciates daily. The result, as with hyperinflation, has been a rise in prices far in excess of the quantity of money. In the first instance, the increase in k exerts a stabilizing price-level effect; in the latter, its decrease a destabilizing blow.

Habits with regard to the use of money, Keynes goes on to observe, may change independently of the quantity of money injected into the system. During recessive phases in the business cycle the value of k, for any given amount of n, tends to grow: expectations of lower prices, in other words, induce more hoarding. For opposite reasons expansions tend to be marked by a fall in k for any given n. This leads to a conclusion which Keynes stresses: given the difficulty in controlling k, a stable quantity of money cannot guarantee stable prices. It follows that in order to stabilize p, n must be manipulated in such a way as to counteract fluctuations in k under different economic situations.[8]

One thing was now clear. The idea that the purchasing power of money is determined by the inviolate rules governing the workings of the economic system is based on an erroneous interpretation of the quantity theory of money in which k is constant and n moves in perfect synchronization with p. If prices and the quantity of money move in unison, and if, as the "healthy" rules of the gold standard suggest, the supply of money rises and falls automatically to balance out the country's foreign accounts, then the purchasing power of money will act to insure the overall equilibrium of the system. Why, then, bother to hinder this spontaneous "natural" action with measures of monetary policy?

A *Tract on Monetary Reform* was undoubtedly a challenge to the concept that money and the price level were neutral with respect to real economic variables. Keynes's analysis of the redistributive effects of inflation and deflation, and of instability of habits in using money, provided a theoretical basis for concrete prescriptions of reform in monetary policy. The traditional theory's corollary that the value of money be allowed to adapt spontaneously to the needs of the balance of payments was equivalent to a pursuit of a stable exchange rate at the expense of domestic price stability. Keynes, on the other hand, argued that avoiding the deleterious effects on real economic variables required a reversal of priorities: prices should be stabilized in lieu of the exchange rate. He recognized thus that price and exchange rate stability were mutually compatible only in certain fortuitous circumstances. According to the purchasing power parity theory, which Keynes conceded as valid under a number of

---

8. Keynes did not consider just the purchasing power held directly by the public in the form of money but also that guaranteed by the public's deposits in the banks. If the real value of these deposits is written as k' and the banking system's reserve coefficient is written as r, the relation proposed by the quantity theory of money becomes $n = p(k + k'r)$. Keynes's observations concerning the variability of k are also valid for k'. To the extent to which they are capable of influencing r the monetary authorities are also capable of stabilizing p, acting either through n or through r.

qualifications, exchange rates reflect the ratio between domestic and foreign prices. Only if the latter remain constant can a country maintain both a stable exchange rate and stable domestic prices. Otherwise one or the other, or both, will bend.

Keynes observed that the creditable performance of the gold standard over a long period of time was due to the lucky coincidence that the discovery of new gold deposits had proceeded at about the same pace as the expansion of economic activity in the West, so that the metal, and thus money, had gone on a parallel track with the system's ability to absorb it. Generalized inflationary pressures had thus been avoided along with deflationary contractions. As far as the future was concerned, however, there was no reason at all to expect that this harmony between the supply of gold and rate of development would continue. Rather it was to be presumed that the supply of gold would essentially depend on the behavior of the handful of countries that controlled the majority of the world's gold reserves, and in particular on gold absorption by the United States. External pressures on sterling and other currencies would thus depend on the policies adopted by the Federal Reserve and by the central banks of a limited group of other countries. To try to hold the gold value of sterling steady at any cost would entail unstable domestic prices.

Keynes's confidence in arguing that domestic prices could be kept stable in the face of a fluctuating sterling exchange rate was very probably due to the specific structure of Britain's foreign trade when Britain could still resort to her colonies for imports of raw materials. This portion of her trade was thus regulated by special currency conditions. At the same time, her exports of manufactured goods were relatively elastic to their dollar price. It could thus be expected that a devaluation of the pound against the dollar, and the consequent depreciation in the gold value of the pound (the gold value of the dollar was constant) would bring the balance of payments back into alignment without creating significant domestic inflationary pressure.

Keynes was not suggesting that the pound be allowed to fluctuate freely. Rather the contrary; he believed that the gold reserves should be deployed to counteract seasonal (or other short-term) fluctuations and that to this end gold should be concentrated in the vaults of the Bank of England. If the central bank's gold reserves were allowed to fluctuate then control over the quantity of money in circulation, and the volume of credit granted by the banks, required a break in any strictly imposed ratio between the gold reserves and the currency issued. In practice, this ratio had been abandoned during both the war and its aftermath. Nonetheless, the British monetary authorities were reluctant to give official sanction to a new system of monetary management; instead there was a certain inclination to return to the prewar system. Hence, as a logical consequence of his pointed analysis, Keynes offered some peremptory prescriptions for British monetary policy:

> Accordingly my first requirement in a good constructive scheme can be supplied merely by a development of our existing arrangements on more deliberate and self-conscious lines. Hitherto the Treasury and the Bank of England have looked forward to the stability of the dollar exchange (preferably at the pre-war parity) as their objective. It is not clear whether they intend to stick to this irrespective of fluctuations in the value of the dollar (or of gold); whether, that is to say, they would sacrifice the stability of sterling prices to the stability of the dollar exchange in the event of the two proving to be incompatible. At any rate, my scheme would require that they should adopt the stability of sterling prices as their *primary* objective—though this would not prevent their aiming at exchange stability also as a secondary objective by co-operating with the Federal Reserve Board in a common policy. So long as the Federal Reserve Board was successful in keeping dollar prices steady the objective of keeping sterling prices steady would be identical with the objective of keeping the dollar-sterling exchange steady. My recommendation does not involve more than a determination that, in the event of the Federal Reserve Board failing to keep dollar prices steady, sterling prices should not, if it could be helped, plunge with them merely for the sake of maintaining a fixed parity of exchange. (P. 147)

Keynes was distressed by the prevailing tendency to minimize, both in theory and in practice, the adverse effects of price level instability. In order to fully understand his preoccupation, one has to bear in mind the official attitudes beginning to be expressed in many Western countries in the early 1920s, involving more or less open support for a "return to gold," and largely to the exchange rates prevailing prior to the abandonment of the gold standard. In the passage quoted above from *A Tract on Monetary Reform*, Keynes alluded to the British authorities' intention to restore the prewar parity of the pound to the dollar. Elsewhere in the book he recalled that at the Conference of Genoa, the Italian, French, and Belgian delegates expressed similar intentions.

The issue of the "return to gold" was distinct from that of the choice between price and exchange-rate stability. The two goals in this latter issue amounted to different ways of adjusting to an imbalance between domestic prices, international prices, and the exchange rate, at times of crisis in the balance of payment. The "return to gold" implied a more cold-blooded monetary decision with the aim of moving from a situation already in equilibrium—with a given level of prices and a given exchange rate—to a new equilibrium with a revalued exchange rate and a deflated price level.

On the choice between price and exchange-rate stability there was still room for debate. Although Keynes had advanced crushing arguments in favor of price stability, a different evaluation of the consequences of price and exchange-rate fluctuations could support different conclusions. What though could possibly justify the idea of restoring prewar parities and simultaneously lowering domestic prices?

Keynes tried to go beyond the trivial answer that the return to gold was motivated by simple-minded nostalgia for the bygone past. He thought he could group the "forces or the reasons" pushing various European countries to revalue their currencies into three main arguments: (1) It was necessary to restore the prewar gold value of the currency so as to repair the injustice committed against those living off rent or off fixed monetary incomes; (2) Restoring a currency's value in gold would increase a country's financial prestige and thus improve expectations for the future (this was a "confidence" factor); and (3) Increasing a currency's gold value would decrease the price of imports and the cost of living, thereby benefiting workers. Also, it would make it easier to pay off foreign debts denominated in gold.

Keynes did not believe any of these arguments to be fully valid; the third he held to be completely mistaken. As far as equity for people on fixed incomes was concerned, he observed that what really mattered for this class was not so much an increase in the gold value of the currency as the resulting fall in domestic prices. Deflation would lead to a huge improvement by a revaluation of rentiers' assets. Given that only a small proportion of these had been accumulated prior to inflation, and that the majority had been formed from the huge volume of gilt-edged stock issued once inflation was already under way, he was skeptical of the "justice" of this improvement.

As for the prestige accruing from devaluation, this argument might hold some weight for countries which succeeded in fully restoring the gold value of their currencies to their prewar levels, but this was only a realistic prospect if they had devalued by less than 5 or 10 percent. Otherwise, it was false to pretend that revaluation would benefit workers by cutting the cost of living; deflation would be bound to affect money wages, and so their purchasing power would remain more or less constant. It was equally false to maintain that revaluation would make it easier to pay off foreign debts denominated in gold: while every pound would buy more dollars (and thus more gold), earning each pound would take more exports. If British goods were to stay competitive, their price in sterling would in fact have to fall.

Keynes's major concern, however, was not with these explicit arguments but rather with their implicit assumptions. Of crucial importance here was the contradiction between his own analysis of the effects of deflation and that implicit in the prevailing theory. A revaluation of the external value of a currency made a general fall in prices and wages inevitable. If it was believed that this implied nothing more than a downward movement in money values without any appreciable effect on production, employment, and investment, a "return to gold" might appear rational, or at any rate a nontraumatic policy decision. Keynes, however, held that a general fall in prices would increase the real burden of debt, setting in motion a process whereby self-fulfilling deflationary expectations would inevitably lead to a fall in production and employment, building in disincentives to accumulation. Given his view, he was bound to see the "return to gold" as a sad calamity for society, brought on by insipid economists and superficial politicians.

CHAPTER 4

CASSANDRA AND THE MYTH
OF THE INVISIBLE HAND

Once again, unfortunately, Keynes was to fulfill his role as Cassandra. Hardly a year had passed since the publication of *A Tract on Monetary Reform* when Winston Churchill, then chancellor of the Exchequer, and the British government decreed that sterling return to its prewar parity of $4.86 = £1. The decision was taken on 28 April 1925. Having abandoned the gold standard in 1914, Britain renewed the tie. The system was not loved; accepted because it had to be, it was to survive until September 1931.

Britain was rapidly followed by Italy. Mussolini announced the decision in a speech at Pesaro. The process that led up to the original historic British decision was not, however, an easy one.[1] The opponents of the move, among whom Keynes naturally played a front-line position, did not succumb without a fight. The final decision for revaluation was rationalized on the basis of a report whose analytical content was, in Keynes's view, completely irrelevant to a reasoned evaluation of the case. The commission that drafted the report had been set up in June 1924 and was composed of experts as highly qualified as Lord Bradbury, Gaspard Farrer, Sir Otto Niemeyer, and Arthur C. Pigou. It was supposed to look into the problem of unifying the issuing of banknotes by the Treasury and by the Bank of England. Keynes was requested to testify on this point. The commission voted merely "to interpret their task so as to include the general question of an immediate return to the gold stan-

---

1. For a complete analysis of British monetary policy during the period 1924–31, see D. E. Moggridge, *British Monetary Policy, 1924–31* (Cambridge: At the University Press, 1972).

dard."[2] The only witness called was Montagu Norman, the governor of the Bank of England and the recognized reigning repository of international central banking (orthodox) wisdom.[3]

Keynes immediately attacked the report in the *Economic Journal*, not hesitating to define it as "a few pages, indolent and jejune."[4] His critique was based not so much on the commission's arguments in favor of revaluation as on problems it had completely ignored. The commission's main argument in favor of a return to gold seemed to be that it was inevitable. The report was devoted to proving that it was not a technical impossibility, and that a parity of $4.79 to £1—the effective exchange rate in February 1925 which some had suggested as the new parity—was in no way preferable to the prewar rate of $4.86. Keynes's note, just six pages long, is a superb example of analytical rigor in facing a reality, which economists thought they had locked away in some golden cages of abstract hypotheses about the neutrality of money.

Proposal for devaluation and "managed money" had been rejected by the commission without discussion. Evaded were a whole series of issues whose importance for stable growth had occupied *A Tract on Monetary Reform*: price stability, prospects for the price of gold, and the risk that the British monetary system might be subordinated to U.S. monetary policy. The Genoa conference's proposals for international cooperation to control cyclical fluctuations in credit, supported by Ralph G. Hawtrey,[5] had also been ignored. The report paid no attention to the possible implications of sterling revaluation for employment and of the domestic deflation necessary to safeguard the balance of payments. Here the weight of orthodoxy swept everything aside.

As already noted this tradition held that a fall in the quantity of money and credit available which led to a general decline of prices would have absolutely no effect on output and jobs. The theory was

---

2. Keynes, "The Committee on the Currency," Notes and Memoranda, *The Economic Journal* (June 1925), p. 299.

3. For an informative biography of Norman, see L. V. Chandler, *Benjamin Strong Central Banker* (Washington, D.C.: The Brookings Institution, 1958), pp. 258–71.

4. "Committee on the Currency," p. 304.

5. Hawtrey, *Monetary Reconstruction* (London: Longmans, 1926).

erected on one implicit, yet crucial hypothesis: that of the downward flexibility of money wages. The presumption was that prices and wages in the different sectors of the economy could fall simultaneously. Hence each individual firm would remain in equilibrium and maintain the same level of production as previously; the system would continue to guarantee a job for anyone willing to work for the prevailing market real wages.

As already observed, Keynes considered a fall in prices as being anything other than neutral. In his attack on the report he did not return to this point; perhaps he assumed that its analytical content could be taken for granted. Rather he focused on the realism of the hypothesis that money wages would fall simultaneously throughout the economy. There was, he observed, a fundamental difference between industries subjected to international competition and domestically "sheltered" industries which were free of world market price stresses. "Unsheltered" industries had to keep their dollar prices in line with international markets; revaluation would thus force them to reduce their prices as expressed in sterling. Sheltered industries were relieved of the bludgeon of foreign competition; revaluation had no direct effect on their prices. Revaluation would thus change the relative prices in the two types of industries and cause crisis in the unsheltered sector forced to lower prices and yet compelled to buy intermediate goods from the sheltered firms at relatively steeper prices. An approximate measure of the gap between these two sets of prices could be detected by comparing the wholesale price index with the index of the cost of living.

How, Keynes asked, did the commission think this gap could be closed? The apparent answer seemed to be through some rise in interest rates and restrictions on credit. It was unclear, however, exactly how a restrictive monetary policy could accomplish the desired impact. Sheltered prices and wages would have to fall, thereby reestablishing the equilibrium that had existed prior to the revaluation. Yet, an increase in the cost of credit would hit both types of industries, creating added troubles for the unsheltered ones. The only way possible to achieve a fall in money wages in the sheltered industries would be through a drastic restrictive monetary policy which would create massive unemployment.[6]

---

6. Here Keynes was thinking of credit rationing.

Unemployment would thus be the final outcome of an economic policy whose effects, in the commission's view, were supposed to be purely monetary:

> I suspect that their conclusions may be based on theories, developed fifty years ago, which assumed a mobility of labour and a competitive wage-level which no longer exist; and that they have not thought the problem through over again in the light of the deplorably inelastic conditions of our industrial organism to-day.[7]

Manifestly, higher interest rates would provoke capital movements, attracting foreign funds and impeding capital outflows. This, in its turn, would alter the balance of payments. Insofar as the improvement on capital account offset the fall in exports there would be an apparent return to "equilibrium"—marred by the gradual decomposition of Britain's exporting industries. There would thus be no need for generalized restrictions on the volume of credit; instead of being spread throughout the system, unemployment would be confined to the weakened sectors most vulnerable to foreign competition. Here, the continuing imbalance between sheltered and unsheltered prices would mean that workers would first be driven to accept lower wages and yet would still end up losing their jobs.

For Britain, which exported capital in the form of direct investment, such a policy would imply a slow death in capital accumulation abroad and in domestic employment, with the gradual destruction of its exporting base. It was very difficult to detect any form of compensation in these joint phenomena. It was therefore impossible to accept the report as containing, in the words of the chancellor of the Exchequer, "a reasoned marshalling of the arguments which have convinced His Majesty's Government."

In July 1925 Keynes presented the arguments of his *Economic Journal* article to a broader public, first in a series of three articles for the *Evening Standard* and then, in greater depth, in a pamphlet entitled *The Economic Consequences of Mr. Churchill*.[8] Here he emphasized the effect of a 10 percent revaluation on the balance of

---

7. Keynes, "Committee on the Currency," p. 302.
8. (London: Hogarth Press, 1925); reprinted in *C.W.K.*, vol. 9.

payments at a time when Britain's prices and wages were already too high compared to her European competitors. He also pointed out the consequences of the inevitable measures of monetary policy on the structure of production and employment.

Inasmuch as world production was at the highest level achieved since 1914, Britain's balance of payments difficulties could hardly be attributed to a lack of world demand. The real problem was relative domestic and international prices. According to many, the complaint was that British prices were high because workers earned too much and produced too little. Keynes observed that while this might be true for certain groups of workers and for specific sectors of industry, it was impossible to argue that all this had happened in the course of the one year during which the foreign trade crisis had emerged and exactly in concert with the revaluation of sterling. It was therefore a simple deduction that unless foreign prices increased at the same rate as prices in Britain the return to gold was bound to discourage exports and encourage imports.

Clearly, an improvement in the balance of payments could not be based, except temporarily, on the improvement in capital account. Such a policy would mean artificially defending the wrong exchange rate and behaving as France did in supporting the franc despite strong criticism in British official circles. What was really imperative was a return to the relative prices in force prior to the revaluation, namely, a 10 percent plunge in British prices. Given that profits in exporting industries—particularly the coal industry—had already been cut to a bare minimum, a fall in wages was crucial. Did the government think this would happen automatically just because it had fixed a new gold parity? The facts were obdurate:

> Our export industries are suffering because they are the first to be asked to accept the 10 per cent reduction. If *every one* was accepting a similar reduction at the same time, the cost of living would fall, so that the lower money wage would represent nearly the same real wage as before. But, in fact, there is no machinery for effecting a simultaneous reduction. Deliberately to raise the value of sterling money in England means, therefore, engaging in a struggle with each separate group in turn, with no prospect that the final result will be fair, and no guarantee that the stronger groups will not gain at the expense of the weaker. . . . Nor can the classes, which are first subjected to a reduction of money wages, be guaranteed that

this will be compensated later by a corresponding fall in the cost of living, and will not accrue to the benefit of some other class. Therefore they are bound to resist so long as they can; and it must be war, until those who are economically weakest are beaten to the ground. (P. 211)

Given the rigidity of money wages, and the impossibility of relying on capital movements, to Keynes the Bank of England was actually moving toward a policy of credit restriction. Although Governor Norman had been careful not to announce such a policy, there had already been a certain reduction in the liquidity available to the clearing banks. This was indeed so effective that an increase in unemployment was already being felt. The bank was already playing the rules of the gold standard game to achieve "the fundamental adjustment." It was evident that the deliberate policy aim was to reduce wages through the creation of an adequate pool of jobless misery.

As already remarked, unemployment was precluded from the logic of orthodox theory, though the latter was prepared to admit that in periods of deflation there might be some "frictional" unemployment owing to the collapse of inefficient firms. It was supposed, however, that after thinning out the least profitable sectors, competition would generate abundant new employment opportunities in more profitable industries. If only allowed to operate freely, the "invisible hand" of capitalism would be bound, ultimately, to reestablish all-around equilibrium. The underlying structure of individual firms would be changed and strengthened.

Keynes's rejection of this image was based both on analytical considerations and on the discernible facts. His analytical objections replicated those raised in *A Tract on Monetary Reform* concerning the destabilizing effects of deflation. As to the real working of the economic system he attached special importance, as noted, to the downward rigidity of money wages.

Superficially, it would seem that he was merely attacking the venerable theoretical proposition that when prices are falling generally, workers will not resist a decline in their money income. But Keynes was really saying something more than this. It was not just a matter of downward wage rigidity; there was a certain skepticism over the effectiveness of relative prices as a means of insuring an optimal allocation of resources and a broader dissatisfaction with the rules of conduct inspired by the principle of laissez-faire and the dubious hypothesis of free competition. This attitude, in my view, was a sign of Keynes's creeping awareness of the characteristics of capitalism at a time when the negative results of the application of theories regardless of the system's specific characteristics were becoming generally apparent.

The question of Keynes's misgivings over the market's spontaneous ability to reallocate resources among different sectors becomes extremely important if we are to interpret correctly his later works, particularly the aggregate format of the *General Theory*. In its dealing with economic variables at a macro level, the *General Theory* has often been taken to concede that at a micro level Keynes implicitly accepted the harmonious functioning of the allocative mechanism. If, however, we view the *General Theory* in the context of his earlier works, this interpretation is definitely incorrect. In *The Economic Consequences of Mr. Churchill*, Keynes's dissatisfaction with the imbalances created by "automatic variations" within individual sectors denotes a value judgment on risks and social costs:

> The truth is that we stand midway between two theories of economic society. The one theory maintains that wages should be fixed by reference to what is "fair" and "reasonable" as between classes. The other theory—the theory of the economic juggernaut—is that wages should be settled by economic pressure, otherwise called "hard facts," and that our vast machine should crash along, with regard only to its equilibrium as a whole, and without attention to the chance consequences of the journey to individual groups.
>
> The gold standard, with its dependence on pure chance, its faith in "automatic adjustments," and its general regardlessness of social detail, is an essential emblem and idol of those who sit in the top tier of the machine. I think that they are immensely rash in their regardlessness, in their vague optimism and comfortable belief that nothing really serious ever happens. Nine times out of ten, nothing really serious does happen—merely a little distress to individuals or to groups. But we run a risk of the tenth time (and are stupid into the bargain), if we continue to apply the principles of an economics, which was worked out on the hypotheses of *laissez-faire* and free competition to a society which is rapidly abandoning these hypotheses. (Pp. 223–24)

Keynes was convinced that spontaneous forces were an unreliable means of restoring equilibrium, even in the microeconomic setting. Less than two years after *The Economic Consequences of Mr. Churchill* he made this view explicit when he suggested measures of industrial policy to resolve the crisis of the Lancashire cotton industry.[9] Given their sales difficulties, the British manufacturers had opted for a general reduction in working hours. Keynes argued that their woes were not due to any lack of world demand for cotton products but rather to the industry's cost structure, which, like the coal industry, had suffered from revaluation. Obviously two years were not enough to allow the industry to restructure itself, reduce its costs, and revive its international viability. Far from being a cure, the slash in working hours risked making the malady far worse. What was needed was direct intervention by a plan agreed to by all the cotton entrepreneurs to close inefficient plants and enhance average productivity. If the entrepreneurs refused to support this kind of plan the government should exert some pressure; the banks should use their control of credit to work in the same direction.

Keynes's attitude toward the principle of laissez-faire and the hypothesis of free competition was revealed even more explicitly in his essay *The End of Laissez-faire*, which was the fruit of two lectures at Oxford University in 1924 and at the University of Berlin in 1926.[10] Here Keynes went so far as to question the origin of the principle that had inspired British liberalism. It was introduced from philosophical utilitarianism into economic thought on the basis of "what the economists are supposed to have said," rather than on the basis of what they had actually said: "No such doctrine is really to be found in the writings of the greatest authorities" (p. 277). There were no scientific grounds for believing the principle to be correct. Nonetheless it was fixed "in the popular mind as the practical conclusion of orthodox political economy" (pp. 279–80). It had penetrated common sense so deeply as to become an article of faith in an economic religion under which "more harm than good is likely to be done by almost any interference of Government with men's money transactions, whether letting and leasing, or buying and selling of any kind."[11]

---

9. For this episode, see Harrod, *Life*, pp. 442–50.

10. (London: Hogarth Press, 1926); reprinted in *C.W.K.* 9.

11. This sentence, quoted by Keynes in ibid., p. 280, is drawn from Archbishop Whately's *Easy Lessons for the Use of Young People*, published in 1850 by the Society for Promoting Christian Knowledge.

According to Keynes the widespread adherence to dogmatic liberalism, with its alleged scientific basis, had influenced the hypotheses proposed by economists in their theories of the capitalist economy. Another reason for their espousal was that they were the simplest hypotheses available; this did not mean, however, they were necessarily valid. Economists had thus accepted as meaningful an account of the market by which the independent behavior of individuals—producers and consumers alike—will insure optimal resource use as they venture by trial and error. In this dynamic process competition insures no mercy for anyone who deploys his energies or capital in the wrong direction. In the "struggle for survival" the success of the efficient goes hand in hand with the bankruptcy of the less capable. The cost of this battle matters not at all; the possibility of mistakes, and waste of resources, is inherent in the power game.

Keynes observed that these analytical propositions on the maximization of overall wealth through the egotistical behavior of individuals depended on hypotheses at odds with reality. It presupposed both the complete independence of production and consumption, and perfect information on market conditions. In reality, individual producers were large enough to influence individual consumers, situations of joint costs were of considerable significance, increasing returns to scale led to a concentration of production, forms of monopoly and collusion prevailed over more competitive behavior, readjustments took a long time, lack of knowledge about market conditions was the general rule. Even economists who recognize the contradiction between their hypotheses and reality remain caught up in their initial assumptions which they suppose as being in some way "natural": "They regard the simplified hypothesis as health, and the future complications as disease."[12]

Keynes also argued in *The End of Laissez-faire* that a great contribution to the success of laissez-faire had come not only from these "text-book" simplifications but also from the implausibility of the two rival doctrines: protectionism and Marxian socialism:

These doctrines are both characterised, not only or chiefly by their infringing the general presumption in favor of *laissez-faire*, but by

---

12. *End of Laissez-faire*, in *C.W.K.* 9:285.

mere logical fallacy. Both are examples of poor thinking, of inability to analyse a process and follow it out to its conclusion. The arguments against them, though reinforced by the principle of *laissez-faire*, do not strictly require it. Of the two, protectionism is at least plausible, and the forces making for its popularity are nothing to wonder at. But Marxian socialism must always remain a portent to the historians of opinion—how a doctrine so illogical and so dull can have exercised so powerful and enduring an influence over the minds of men and, through them, the events of history. (P. 285)

At this point it is intriguing to conjecture on Keynes's evolving intuition and attitude toward capitalism. Innately, on reason and observation, he resisted the classical canons of unbonded individualism: To what degree did he think that the capitalist economic organization of society should be modified? Certainly there can be no doubt that in the broadest sense Keynes extolled human freedom and dignity, and that he believed that these, on the whole, were best attended to by private capital accumulation. Those who profess otherwise are guilty of misrepresenting his deepest ideological roots.

His whole analysis of the workings of the system would have been pointless if he had completely rejected private enterprise. From his meditations in *A Short View of Russia* it seems appropriate to conclude that while he accepted capitalism for its efficiency in attaining broad socially impeccable goals he rejected some of it as a system of values. *The End of Laissez-faire* confirms this attitude:

Confusion of thought and feeling leads to confusion of speech. Many people, who are really objecting to capitalism as a way of life, argue as though they were objecting to it on the ground of its inefficiency in attaining its own objects. . . .

Nevertheless, a time may be coming when we shall get clearer than at present as to when we are talking about capitalism as an efficient or inefficient technique, and when we are talking about it as desirable or objectionable in itself. For my part I think that capitalism, wisely managed, can probably be made more efficient for attaining economic ends than any alternative system yet in sight, but that in itself it is in many ways extremely objectionable. Our problem is to work out a social organisation which shall be as efficient as possible without offending our notions of a satisfactory way of life. (Pp. 293–94)

What did "a wise management" of capitalism intend? In what sectors should private enterprise apply? Did Keynes wish the state to intervene indiscriminately as some unsympathetic interpreters imply? Here again it is worth letting Keynes offer his own reply:

> The most important *Agenda* of the State relate not to those activities which private individuals are already fulfilling, but to those functions which fall outside the sphere of the individual, to those decisions which are made by *no one* if the State does not make them. The important thing for government is not to do things which individuals are doing already, and to do them a little better or a little worse; but to do those things which at present are not done at all. (P. 291)

On the matter of the scope of state interventions Keynes mentions three areas, as examples. The subsequent rendition of Keynes's thought reveals, however, that these examples were not chosen at random. The first example, suggested by intuition, was that "many of the greatest economic evils of our time are the fruits of risk, uncertainty, and ignorance" (p. 291).

There was no way individuals could remedy these obstacles; many private operators actually prospered in circumstances that tended to turn major enterprise into a "lottery." State intervention could thus take the form of central bank management over money and credit. The state too should help to make the market transparent through the collection and dissemination of data on market facts.

Second, savings and credit could not be left wholly unfettered. The state had to estimate the desirable volume of community savings and the proportion to be directed to foreign investment, and it had to aid the private capital market to deflect the funds into channels most profitable to society.

Third, the state ought to have a clear policy on optimal population size and ought to consider how best, without coercion, to implement this objective. Ultimately the community had to concern itself collectively not only with the number but also the "quality" of the population.

What political climate would be most hospitable to this turnabout in the concept of the role of the state? In the summer of 1925 Keynes gave a lecture to the Liberal Summer School in Cambridge with the significant title "Am I a Liberal?".[13] In this lecture Keynes outlined his basic philosophy of an "ideal party," leaving it up to his audience to decide whether this could be fitted into the ideology of the British Liberal party. In this lecture we find the central argument put forward in *The End of Laissez-faire*, namely, that contemporary reality made the idea of an invisible hand an anachronism. We also find support for an explicit model of the phases in the historical development of capitalism, attributed to John Commons. According to this model, after an initial period of scarcity, lasting from the fifteenth to the sixteenth century, there followed a period of abundance, culminating in the nineteenth century. Now capitalism had entered a third phase, and, if it was going to survive, it needed a period of recuperative "stabilization." This required some limitation on individual economic freedom and a growth in the role of concerted action by unions and employers associations (p. 304). According to Keynes a climate of public opinion was coming into being that would favor acceptance of contributory measures to make stabilization feasible:

> The trade unions are strong enough to interfere with the free play of the forces of supply and demand, and public opinion, albeit with a grumble and with more than a suspicion that the trade unions are growing dangerous, supports the trade unions in their main contention that coal-miners ought not to be the victims of cruel economic forces which they *never* set in motion. (P. 305)

He was also aware, however, that the tasks to be fulfilled in this third phase of capitalism were such that everyone, and particularly economists, would have to draw on their deepest resources of initiative and imagination: "We have to invent new wisdom for a new age. And in the meantime we must, if we are to do any good, appear unorthodox, troublesome, dangerous, disobedient to them that begat us" (p. 306).

---

13. *Nation and Athenaeum*, 8 and 15 August 1925; reprinted in *C.W.K.*, vol. 9.

PART 2

THE OUTLINE
OF A GENERAL THEORY

CHAPTER 5

MONEY, PROFITS, AND PRICES UNDER FULL EMPLOYMENT

Difficult years followed Britain's decision to return to gold. After the brief boom of 1924 unemployment increased persistently. The government, by devaluing sterling, had forced itself into a deflation corner; the monetary policy of the Bank of England, fully coherent with the government line, was to darken the situation. In the spring of 1926 came the crisis in the coal industry, which with its low profit margins had been the unsheltered industry most exposed to revaluation. Bearing in mind the competition of German and Polish coal on the European market, no other exporting industry was in more dire need of a cut in production costs. Unfortunately, any hope of greater productivity, at least in the short term, was considered illusory. The mine owners and the Conservative government insisted on slashing money wages, and the miners proclaimed an all-out strike with the other unions joined in solidarity. Thus, the first General Strike in the history of British trade unionism shook the country to its roots.

The Lancashire cotton industry was also in distress, its exports having fallen to a level insufficient to absorb production. As mentioned earlier, the employers' solution was a cut in working hours, with spreading underemployment rather than unemployment proper. The crisis was becoming unrestrained. Before the General Elections in the spring of 1929 Keynes estimated that unemployment hovered at one million.[1] The pending collapse of Wall Street aggravated the crisis enormously, pushing back the potential date for concrete recovery.

---

1. Keynes, in collaboration with H. Henderson, "Can Lloyd George Do It?" (1929); reprinted in *C.W.K.*, vol. 9.

This, in outline, was the gravity of the British situation in the stormy period between 1926 and 1930 when Keynes wrote *A Treatise on Money*, published in two volumes in October 1930.[2] This work was the fruit of Keynes's most ambitious undertaking in the field of monetary theory, being a theoretical synthesis derived from his concrete personal experience with capitalism up to that time. Although I do not wish to detract from the importance of *A Tract of Monetary Reform*, it is nevertheless the *Treatise* which represents Keynes's original flowering contribution to the understanding of the role of money. Keynes's aim, in fact, was to resolve problems previously left dangling. The theoretical significance of the *Treatise* is that it is a juncture in the process whereby Keynes sought a rational, analytical description, at a high level of abstraction, of the capitalist reality which he had encountered so long at the empirical level.

The main argument of *A Tract on Monetary Reform* revolved about the non-neutral nature of fluctuations in the purchasing power of money on real economic magnitudes. Accordingly, the proper aim of monetary policy was to manipulate the money supply so as to maintain a stable price level. It followed that the "healthy rules" of conduct inspired by the gold standard and the faith in the "invisible hand" were misplaced and ought to be revised. Under downward rigidity in wages, or in a situation in which different sectors of the economy showed discrepancies in their ability to resist domestic and foreign competition, rational conduct made it incumbent on the central bank to manipulate the availability of credit so as to create unemployment: job deflation was the only way to align money wages with prices.[3]

In order for Keynes's propositions to achieve analytical coherence it was first necessary to demolish the quantity theory of money, in either the Cambridge or the Irving Fisher equational versions.[4] If Keynes could show that there existed independent nonmonetary

---

2. (London: Macmillan); reprinted in *C.W.K.*, vols. 5 and 6.

3. In our day the strongest supporter, in the tradition of Keynes, of inducing the alignment through incomes policy, has been Sidney Weintraub. See, e.g., his *Capitalism, Inflation and Unemployment Crisis: Beyond Monetarism and Keynesianism* (Reading, Pa.: Addison-Wesley, 1978), chaps. 3–9.

4. Fisher, *The Purchasing Power of Money* (New York: Macmillan, 1911).

elements capable of disturbing prices, then the task of monetary policy had to be that of preventing these forces from gathering strength. Ineluctably, he first had to sever the rigid quantity theory proportionality knot between the price level and the money supply.

Keynes had already demonstrated the variability in the amount of purchasing power held in liquid form during periods of expansion and recession (variations in the velocity of the circulation of money), and he had referred explicity, as was his style, to the way in which prices and money circulation varied empirically during the different phases in the business cycle. What remained, however, was to expose the endogenous causes of variations in the price level; all he had done so far was to take fluctuations in the purchasing power of money as a fact and to concentrate on their effect on the overall balance of the system. To give a rigorous demonstration of the rationality of a new mission to entrust to monetary policy it was crucial to identify the mechanisms responsible for fluctuations in the price level and the relationship between these mechanisms and the behavior of the monetary institutions.

A clearer definition of this aspect of the question was essential in order to elaborate how manipulation of the money supply could impinge on prices and money wages once the strict quantity theory proportionality was rejected on analytical grounds and unemployment induced wage compression for social reasons.

The core of the *Treatise on Money* consists of an analysis in depth of the factors responsible for fluctuations in the purchasing power of money and the channels through which monetary policy influences prices and money wages. It thus seems that from 1925 on Keynes concentrated precisely on those problems he had escaped in the *Tract on Monetary Reform*. His more ambitious program now was to explore the monetary cycle.

Keynes's original contribution to monetary theory is contained in books 3 and 4 (volume 1) of the *Treatise*. Book 3, dedicated to the "fundamental equations," opens by defining several macroeconomic aggregates, namely, income, profit, and savings and investment. Keynes was not to use until later these variables, but he wanted to specify their content in relation to the special definition he used for "profits."

As usually defined, profit is a component of income. Keynes's notion of income, however, included salaries and wages, interest on capital, gains from monopoly and rent, as well as a "normal return to entrepreneurs," and excluded all "abnormal" profits (or losses) above interest on capital and the entrepreneurs' "normal return." According to Keynes's definition, profits consist of the (positive or negative) difference between the aggregative income from sales and the sum of the "cost" paid to the factors listed above. As unexpected gains, "abnormal" profits are excluded from the notion of income. Savings are defined as the difference between the community's income and its expenditure on consumption. Savings and profits are the source of every increase in a nation's wealth. Investment is defined as the net increase in capital stock over a given period of time; the value of investment is taken as the value of this increase.

Keynes's purpose in formulating his "fundamental equations for the value of money" was clearly set out in his introduction:

> The fundamental problem of monetary theory is not merely to establish identities or statistical equations relating (e.g.) the turnover of monetary instruments to the turnover of things traded for money. The real task of such a theory is to treat the problem dynamically, analysing the different elements involved, in such a manner as to exhibit the causal process by which the price level is determined, and the method of transition from one position of equilibrium to another. The forms of the quantity theory, however, on which we have all been brought up . . . are but ill adapted for this purpose. They are particular examples of the numerous identities which can be formulated connecting different monetary factors. But they do not, any of them, have the advantage of separating out those factors through which, in a modern economic system, the causal process actually operates during a period of change. (P. 120)

Methodologically, Keynes fell short of a clear distinction between dynamic intention and his actual method, which was largely an exercise in comparative statics. Nonetheless, Keynes intuitively continued to pinpoint the quantity theory of money as an essential theoretical anchor. His goal was to unravel the Cambridge equation into other fundamental macroeconomic variables, and ultimately to establish a precise relationship between the price level and its determinants. To this end he designates the monetary income of the nation as E, and the income earned by the productive factors engaged in producing investment goods as I': this is thus the value of investment, measured in terms of production costs, while $E - I'$

represents the production cost of consumer goods. If savings are denoted by the symbol S, then $E - S$ measures current consumption expenditure.

Keynes goes on to adopt a unit of measurement for output so that one unit of each good has an equal cost of production at the beginning of the period under consideration. Total production in terms of this unit, in each time interval, is written as O; R shows the flow of production of goods and services purchased by consumers; C signifies the flow of net investment. Thus: $O = R+C$. If P represents the price level of consumer goods, PR equals current expenditure on consumption, or the difference between income and savings. From $I' = E(C/O)$ it follows that

$$PR = E - S = (E/O)(R + C) - S = (E/O)R + I' - S.$$

From this equation Keynes derives the price level of consumer goods P:

$$P = \frac{E}{O} + \frac{I' - S}{R}. \tag{i}$$

Equation (i) is the first of the "fundamental equations" of the *Treatise*. The term E/O expresses the unit cost of production shown by W_1. If W is the monetary cost per factor unit and if e represents an index of overall productivity (Keynes's "coefficient of efficiency"), so that $W_1 = W/e$, equation (i) may be written:

$$P = W_1 + \frac{I' - S}{R}$$

or

$$P = \frac{1}{e}W + \frac{I' - S}{R}.$$

The price level for consumer goods is thus determined by the sum of the unit cost of production and the unit gap between the cost of total investment and the volume of savings. Only when prices and unit costs of production are equal does investment, in terms of production costs, equal savings.

The possibility of a discrepancy between prices and unit costs of production was undoubtedly the most original aspect of Keynes's analysis. Compared to the rigid approach of the quantity theory, the argument that the consumer price level moved with the gap between investment and savings—two real magnitudes—was indeed provocative. It was to become the major target for Keynes's critics.

Keynes explains the gap between investment and savings as follows. Total output consists of a certain quantity of consumer goods and a certain quantity of investment goods. The income received by the factors of production employed in these two sectors is partly spent on consumption and partly saved, but:

> the division of the output between investment and goods for consumption is not necessarily the same as the division of the income between savings and expenditure on consumption. For workers are paid just as much when they are producing for investment as when they are producing for consumption; but having earned their wages, it is they who please themselves whether they spend or refrain from spending them on consumption. Meanwhile, the entrepreneurs have been deciding quite independently in what proportions they shall produce the two categories of output. (P. 123)

Given this separation between decisions to produce and decisions to consume, it is a pure coincidence if supply and demand for consumer goods balance out at a price equal to their cost of production. This, however, is equivalent to saying that it is a happy concurrence if $I' - S = 0$. Any discrepancy of $(I' - S) \gtrless 0$, or between expenditure on consumption and the cost value of the consumption goods produced, is bound to generate a gap between the cost value of investment and savings. To illustrate, using Keynes's notation to express the identity between the source and the destination of income:

$$I' + E - I' = PR + S.$$

If $PR > E - I'$, it follows that $I' > S$ given that $PR - (E - I') = I' - S$. Suppose that this situation arises, that at a price level $P = W_1$ the sum which income-earners wish to spend on consumption outweighs the cost value of consumption goods. P will thus be pushed upward until the fall in the purchasing power of the sum spent on consumption is sufficient to match the demand for consumer goods with the volume actually produced. But this implies a gap between total sales receipts and total production costs, which Keynes defines as profit. The positive or negative gap between I' and S is thus synonymous with profits or losses for the producers of consumer goods.

The first fundamental equation may thus be interpreted to state that the price level for consumer goods is equal to their cost in the absence of profits, and that it outruns cost when profits emerge. Keynes's thought is that profits (or losses) tend to encourage (or discourage) production, thereby altering the magnitudes under scrutiny. Hence the only condition for equilibrium—in the sense of nil pressure for change—is when profits are zero. Equilibrium implies that the price level equals the unit cost of production.[5]

From certain of Keynes's considerations concerning the effects of decisions to spend a part or the whole of profits on consumption, one may derive a hypothesis never clearly expressed in the first fundamental equation, namely, that *real income is a constant*. If entrepreneurs divert their profits to consumption rather than to accumulating wealth, this increases consumption and cuts savings. This implies that real income is in no way modified by variations in decisions to spend, and the first fundamental equation leads to the conclusion that a decline in S enlarges the difference $I' - S$, that is, it augments the profit of the consumer goods sector. Since changes in wealth are engendered by the sum of savings and profits, it follows that spending a portion of profits on consumption is neutral on the formation of new wealth, that is, any fall in savings is exactly compensated by a profit rise in the consumer goods sector. On the other hand, when entrepreneurs suffer losses and react by cutting their consumption, the consequent surge in savings imposes equivalent losses on the producers of consumer goods.

Keynes explains that

> however much of their profits entrepreneurs spend on consumption, the increment of wealth belonging to entrepreneurs remains the same as before. Thus profits, as a source of capital increment for entrepreneurs, are a widow's cruse which remains undepleted however much of them may be devoted to riotous living. When, on the other hand, entrepreneurs are making losses, and seek to recoup these losses by curtailing their normal expenditure on consumption, i.e. by saving

---

5. Note that the adjustment process is here entirely based on prices, whereas the mechanism in the *General Theory* will rest mainly on output variations.

more, the cruse becomes a Danaid jar which can never be filled up.
(P. 125)

In the logical process Keynes applies to elicit the price level
for consumer goods he completely ignores the price level for investment goods. Given that the capital goods prices obviously influence decisions concerning the quantity produced, and thus the value
of I' and P, the approach entails the ubiquitous *coeteris paribus*.
Implicitly, the first fundamental equation presupposes that investment goods prices are given.

For Keynes this analytical isolation of the forces that determine the two price levels was more than a simplifying procedure
based on successive stages of approximation. The logic used to explain investment goods prices deviates sharply from that covering
consumer goods. No longer is this logic tied to production costs but
rather, and tightly so, to *financial decisions taken by savers and by
the banking system.*

Keynes observes that the decision to save a portion of income
implies a further decision on the financial form in which the savings
are to be held. For simplicity he subdivides the different possible
forms of savings into bank deposits and equity shares. The willingness to hold one or the other of these assets depends not only on
savers' preferences but also on the rate of interest on deposits and
the price of, and thus the return to, shares.[6] The choice between
the two assets concerns not only the ultimate financial destination
of savings flows but also the composition of the entire stock of wealth,
a limited portion of which emanates from savings over a given period of time. Given the stock composition of wealth, the price of
shares thus depends on the preference of the public and on the rate
of interest on bank deposits or, to be more precise, on the behavior
of the banking system with respect to the supply of deposits and
the demand for shares. Keynes ties the price of shares to the price
of investment goods, seeing the two as very closely linked. He thus
concludes: "the actual price level of investment is the resultant of

---

6. Surely here Keynes deserves some recognition for his precocity
in anticipating modern portfolio-theory, as developed in the present era
by James Tobin, among others. See Tobin, "Money, Capital and Other
Stores of Value," *American Economic Review*, Papers and Proceedings,
May 1961, and "A General Equilibrium Approach to Monetary Theory,"
Journal of Money, Credit and Banking, February 1969.

the sentiment of the public and the behaviour of the banking system."[7]

Symbolically, let I represent investment and P' represent the price level for investment goods, with $I = P'C$ the market *value* of the aggregate quantity produced (as distinct from the cost of production I') over a definite time interval. If Π is the price level for *both* consumer and investment goods, then:

$$\Pi = \frac{PR + P'C}{R + C} = \frac{(E-S) + I}{O} = \frac{E}{O} + \frac{I-S}{O}. \tag{ii}$$

This is the "second fundamental equation" of the *Treatise*. It declares that the average price level for the whole system can depart from the unit cost of production ($E/O = W_1$) by the discrepancy between the market value of investment and the volume of savings. Profits realized by the investment goods sectors (noted by Q_2) amount to the difference between the market value of investment and its cost. Symbolically:

$$Q_2 = I - I'.$$

The profits realized by the consumer goods sector, signified by Q_1, have already been revealed as

$$Q_1 = I' - S.$$

Therefore, with Q representing total profit then:

$$Q = Q_1 + Q_2 = I - S.$$

Manifestly, it follows that like P, the average price level Π is equivalent to production costs only if total profits are zero.

Despite the different forces and mechanisms, the two price levels P and P' interreact. High prices for investment goods, for instance, exert a positive effect on profits in this sector, thereby influencing production, I', and consumer goods prices. As a result, all the different factors that change P' (the financial decisions by the public and the bank) indirectly lead to changes in P. On the other hand, the price level of consumer goods, and above all the expectations to which this gives rise, may influence the public's financial options and thus P'.

---

7. *Treatise* in *C.W.K.* 5:128.

To assess the degree of heresy embodied in Keynes's equational analysis of the purchasing power of money one must compare it with the unequivocal relationship between money and price level variations propounded in the quantity theory of money. The fundamental equations of the *Treatise* lay bare a whole series of transmission factors capable of changing the average price level Π (and the purchasing power reciprocal $1/\Pi$) even when money supplies remain constant. Preferences, behavioral patterns, and decisions move profits and therefore prices. If the *Treatise* stopped here we might conclude that what we were treated to was but a complicated explanation of a variety of factors capable of modifying the velocity of money. Compared to a rigid quantity theory, Keynes's explanation might then have been judged as mostly killing the idea that money is just a veil concealing real magnitudes with respect to which its action is neutral. Nonetheless, it would have been nothing more than an extended and improved version of the analysis in *A Tract on Monetary Reform*.

The deeper perception is that Keynes was struggling to isolate the elusive transmission mechanism—still unresolved since Richard Cantillon's brilliant exposé in 1732—through which money augmentations affect prices, wages, and employment. While the fundamental equations are merely a tool of analysis, admiration must extend to the way in which Keynes deploys the equations to grapple with the problem. The issue impels some concentrated attention.

In an economy with a banking system an increase in the money supply involves a willingness by the banks to grant credit on more favorable terms than previously. For Keynes the positive effect on investment of a decrease in interest on bank loans consists of some bulge in the price level for investment goods P'. More profit ensues in this sector, thereby stimulating the production of investment goods C. At the same time, the fall in interest rates, once it spreads to the whole range of financial assets, discourages saving. For both these reasons, the discrepancy of $I' - S$ increases and thus inflates P, the price level for consumer goods. If profits (or losses) operate to modify the liquid reserves and current account deposits which entrepreneurs seek to hold as a means of payment in the same way as payment flows to factors of production do, then in the consumer goods sector profit creation would absorb the initial advance in the quantity of money and the process would grind to a halt.

Keynes's hypothesis, however, is that the variation in liquid reserves induced by profits (or losses) is less than that caused by changes in money incomes. The process may thus be replicated, and so the next stage consists of the consumer goods producers' reaction to the positive profit: $Q_1 = (I' - S) > 0$.

Profits stimulate production; the entrepreneurs compete in the market for available factors, provoking an increase in their remuneration. The increase in $(I' - S)$, contained in the first fundamental equation, is transmitted to W_1; the creation of profits compels, in other words, some advance in the unit cost of production. This evokes an increase in the need for liquid reserves (that is, money in the "industrial circulation"), eroding the general liquidity of the system: the banks ultimately must smother the economic expansion. The investment level achieved previously is retarded, savings are increased by the upturn in interest rates, and profits in the consumer sector $(I' - S)$ fall. A new equilibrium is reached, Keynes concludes, when profits become nil and the price level P and the unit cost W_1 adapt to the increased quantity of money.

In the last analysis, will the rise in the price level exactly match the jump in the quantity of money, or will the money cause and price resultant differ? If in the transition from the initial to the final equilibrium there are no changes in: (1) real income, (2) employment, (3) habits concerning the holding of liquid reserves, (4) the financial preferences of the public, or (5) the behavior of the banking system, then the price level will change in strict proportion to the quantity of money. The quantity theory of money thus retains its validity but only under these provisos, namely, within a framework where nothing is supposed to change—except money—and then observing that nothing does change but prices.

In retrospect it is possible to fudge the heuristic value of the analysis as extremely limited: the *Treatise* did not shake the foundations of the quantity theory. This, however, was not Keynes's objective. Rather, he was trying to trace the path by which money alters real variables, and the tasks thus to be assigned to monetary policy in order to stabilize prices. From this standpoint he had undoubtedly come a considerable distance from the *Tract*. It was now apparent that the channel through which monetary policy could influence the price level was a discrepancy between investment and savings. To this purpose the monetary authorities had to push the effective market rate of interest above or below the level necessary to balance investment and savings—what Keynes, borrowing Knut Wicksell's terminology, called the "natural rate."

It has been shown, however, that achieving a new price equilibrium after the initial perturbation associated with the emergence of profits (or losses) requires a change in the unit cost of production. Further, this change has to be induced by a modified entrepreneurs' demand for factors of production, under the stimulus of profits (or losses):

> For the departure of profits from zero is the mainspring of change in the industrial countries of the modern world outside Russia. It is by altering the rate of profits in particular directions that entrepreneurs can be induced to produce this rather than that, and it is by altering the rate of profits in general that they can be induced to modify the average of their offers of remuneration to the factors of production.[8]

The conclusions reached in *A Tract on Monetary Reform* are thus confirmed. The only way in which a deflationary monetary policy can achieve its ends is by reducing firms' demands for factors. Now, however, Keynes's analysis has become more rigorous and more general in scope, making it clear that if the monetary authorities aim to deflate prices when unit costs of production are rising, by virtue of a hike in money wages or downturn in productivity, the task facing them becomes formidable. Beyond halting the cost pressure they would actually have to reverse the autonomous cost upticks. This might well entail an artificial burst of savings over investment, or a cold-blooded blow inflicting heavy losses on entrepreneurs.

The analysis of deflation in the *Treatise* also demonstrates that despite Keynes's suggestions in his less rigorous approach of the mid-1920s, unemployment finds no haven in a general theory in which real income is a datum. Keynes still insists on the possibility of monetary wages remaining frozen despite a fall in the demand for labor, thereby causing a fall in employment. Yet he sees this as a temporary phenomenon, as a disequilibrium which, even if protracted, is bound to culminate in a new equilibrium with prices and wages neatly adapted to the quantity of money:

> A change in the quantity of money will change the rate of investment; the change in the rate of investment will bring with it profit or loss; and the stimulus of profit or loss, if carried far enough and continued long enough, will change sooner or later the average rate

8. Ibid., p. 141.

of earnings; and at long last the change in individual rates of earnings will again conform appropriately to the change in the average rate of earnings, instead of being dispersed inequitably about the average as they will be at first and perhaps for a period of years. (Pp. 243–44)

There is a world of difference between a manipulation of the money supply to control a price level threatened by upheaval in the unit cost of production, and money maneuvers aimed at choking inflationary or deflationary shocks that are due to discrepancies between investment and savings. Keynes's judgment was strongly hostile on the invocation of monetary policy to cope with what we now call "cost inflation."[9] If the unit cost of production moves up autonomously, monetary policy could only destabilize the system by imposing a wedge between the market and the "natural" rate of interest; other direct and less destructive tools of economic policy would have to be devised.

On the other hand, in the presence of a spontaneously creeping discrepancy between investment and savings—what we would now call "demand inflation"[10]—Keynes believed that price stabilization could then be entrusted to monetary policy, striving to align the market with the natural interest rate. The rolling sequence of phases of excessive investment and excessive savings constituted Keynes's version of the "credit cycle." Although he recognized that this kind of price oscillation could destabilize unit costs, or the presence of a reverse feedback, he considered it theoretically and practically important (from the standpoint of monetary policy) to envision these sources of disequilibrium as being analytically independent "provided that the initial impulse comes from investment disequilibria and the costs of production are a reaction to these disequilibria and not to some independent or lasting change in the monetary situation."[11]

Keynes had earlier delved into the extreme volatility of the capital accumulation process in *The Economic Consequences of the Peace*. In the *Treatise* this instability comes in the form of sudden changes in the decisions taken by producers of investment goods. In industrialized economies the first phase of the credit cycle usually begins in this way. Consider, for example, an investment in-

9. Keynes calls this *income inflation*.
10. Keynes speaks here of *commodity inflation* (or *deflation*).
11. *Treatise* in C.W.K. 5:249.

crease induced by better profit prospects in the investment goods sector, achieved at the expense of consumer goods output. Specifying decisions to save as completely independent of decisions to invest, and that both are usually relatively stable, the result will be an outcome in which investment outruns savings. The excess demand for consumer goods may put pressure on their relative prices, with a blowup in factor remuneration if the shift of resources from consumer to investment goods involves competition among entrepreneurs. Anyway, the essential characteristic of this first cyclical phase will be a lift in the price level with respect to costs: positive profits will emerge. The cost creep can be covered by draining the public's reserves of liquid cash, fostered by the gradual spread of the expansionary climate.

The mechanism in the second phase of the credit cycle resembles the scenario of an initial increase in the money supply. Profit stimulates production with an increased demand for factors topped off by higher factor remuneration and production costs. The final equilibrium, however, is altogether different, for there is no initial swell in the quantity of money to support the cost hike. The liquidity shortage presses banks to up the interest rate. Investment thus drops below its initial level; not only are profits erased but savings overcome investment. As a result expansion degenerates into a recession phase, with lower demand for factors and the reduction of unit costs to the initial level so that prices also resume their original gait.

Meantime, in the adjustment interval the system is shaken by a series of destabilizing features which, because of rigidities and friction, induce unemployment and erect a discontinuous accumulation stress. The most important task of monetary policy should be to stifle this cycle at the outset.

CHAPTER 6

ORTHODOXY AND HERESY IN
A TREATISE ON MONEY

This chapter is devoted to some reflection on Keynes's *Treatise* analysis, considering certain irresolutions and appraising the significance of the theory as an interpretation of capitalism marking a bold step beyond the traditional theory.

First, to what extent does the analytical core of the *Treatise* correspond with the vision of capitalism contained in Keynes's earlier works? What I have in mind in particular is that part of *The Economic Consequences of the Peace* in which Keynes so effectively seized on the central volatility of the capitalist system, namely, the extreme instability of its capital accumulation mechanism. In a long-term historical perspective he saw both the continuity and the disruption ratchet. From this grand vision one would expect an analysis emanating from the same themes established by classical economics,[1] that is, the long-term relationship between growth and capital accumulation, and between capital accumulation and the rate of profit. Instead, Keynes's analytic fulcrum goes off to the relationship between money and the price level, with the methodological priority sited in the short term. In the background, out of focus, we barely perceive the growth and accumulation theme. Even further off we catch a glimpse of income distribution, deliberately excluded from the *Treatise*.[2]

---

1. By classical economics I am referring to the development of economic thinking from Adam Smith to Karl Marx. Keynes, on the other hand, used this term more extensively in the *General Theory* to characterize practically all of his eminent predecessors, at Cambridge and elsewhere.

2. See the passage at p. 151 of the *Treatise* (in *C.W.K.*, vol. 5) in which Keynes declares that he cannot concern himself with autonomous movements in wages.

Quite apart from these immediate impressions on the *Treatise*, a calibration of the degree of harmony between Keynes's vision of capitalism and his theoretical model entails two separate layers of judgment. For instance, one is bound to distinguish the analytic method from the content of the theory. The *Economic Consequences of the Peace*, and certain sections of the *Tract on Monetary Reform*, seem to invoke an analysis capable of identifying the fundamental forces driving the capitalist order, a method in which the evaluation of the historical significance of phenomena is an integral part of the theory. This was the method of classical economics, a method characteristic of David Ricardo and Karl Marx and latent, though with less purity, in Adam Smith.[3] Classical analysis hinged on the theory of value: the attempt to identify the forces that determine, in the capitalist method of production, the long-term exchange relationships among commodities. Theories of distribution, growth, and crisis were integral parts of this theory which constituted a vision of reality centered on a unifying concept: the labor content of commodities.

By the time Keynes was elaborating the monetary theory of the *Treatise*, the unchallenged dominant doctrines were no longer those of the classical economists but direct descendants of the "marginalist revolution" of William S. Jevons, Carl Menger, and Leon Walras, as subsequently refined by Marshall. This method—Marshall's neoclassical synthesis—had ousted the classical mode and disavowed any significant distinction between the fundamental and the immediate determinants of the exchange relationship, transforming value theory into a theory of prices. Here, income distribution was no longer the result of a social dialectic stemming from the production organization of capitalist society; rather it came to be unequivocally determined by productivity, by techniques of production taken as data. Above all, the neoclassical method shook off any reference to the specific historical and institutional characteristics of the economic system which was meant to be the object of the analysis. Instead, it based its conclusions on an abstract system of rational individuals in which "rationality" was made synonymous with the maximization of utility and profit.

---

3. For a recent vigorous presentation of the method of the classical economics, see N. De Vecchi, *Valore e profitto nell'economia politica classica* (Milan: Feltrinelli, 1976).

The transition from the classical theory to the neoclassical synthesis implied much more than just a change of method: in fact the theory lost its content. The aim was no longer to analyze capitalism's growth and crises but rather to depict an abstract system in which everything depends on everything else in a model of simultaneous equations "proving" a theoretical general economic equilibrium.

It follows that if the *Treatise* (and the *Tract*) were molded on the neoclassical model, it would be pointless to distinguish between the method and the content of the theory. Nonetheless, the distinction is valid. Although Keynes was incapable of applying the classical structure to his analysis of capitalism, he was absolutely unwilling to abandon his search for a theoretical explanation of the concrete phenomena which his experience as an empirical economist had forced on him.[4]

The rather puzzling heterodox content of the *Treatise* makes it legitimate to query the residual influence of Marshall, Keynes's old mentor. Marshall's impact has often been discerned to ramify beyond his great *Principles of Economics*[5] to Keynes's work of the 1920s which indubitably relies on partial equilibrium analysis. While I do not deny this methodological linkage, it will not be the focal point of attention.

Marshall's work has been pinpointed as an attempt at an eclectic compromise between the classical economists and the viewpoint inspired by the marginalist revolution. How far this wedlock was fruitful remains, nearly a century later, a point of contention.[6] My own view is that one of its basic ingredients was Marshall's unwavering insistence, in edition after edition of the *Principles*, in envisioning the problems of industry and business as the analytic object of the theory of production. This search for concreteness and economic reality must surely have encouraged Keynes's own vow to

---

4. The same general assessment appears in a very clear essay delivered by G. Lunghini to the 16th meeting of the Società Italiana degli Economisti and published as *La crisi dell'economia politica e la teoria del valore* (Milan: Feltrinelli, 1977).

5. 8th ed. (London: Macmillan, 1920).

6. See the many issues thrown up in G. Becattini's broad-ranging introduction to the Italian edition of Alfred Marshall and Mary P. Marshall's early (1879) *The Economics of Production* (*Economia della produzione* [Milan: ISEDI, 1975]).

avoid the dangerous, yet academically attractive routes of abstract theorizing. Significant here are Keynes's comments in his obituary on Marshall in the *Economic Journal*, even defending Marshall's habit of systematically procrastinating in publishing his work:

> Marshall . . . arrived very early at the point of view that the bare bones of economic theory are not worth much in themselves and do not carry one far in the direction of useful, practical conclusions. The whole point lies in applying them to the interpretation of current economic life. This requires a profound knowledge of the actual facts of industry and trade. But these, and the relation of individual men to them, are constantly and rapidly changing.[7]

Keynes's academic training had been entirely conventional and orthodox in the manner expected of a Cambridge scion. The economic issues he was confronted with were, however, quite heterodox. This carried a risk, namely, that the inadequate analytical tools at hand would obstruct him in attaining a sufficiently rigorous assessment of the phenomena he was studying. He ran this risk and, undoubtedly, paid the price in the *Treatise*.

The analytic core of volume 1 of the *Treatise* has already been outlined. The puzzle that Keynes intended to face here was that of capitalism's chronic cyclical crises, highlighted concretely in the inflationary and deflationary sequences of the 1920s. For Keynes, the whole crisis theme was closely tied in with that of the instability of the capital accumulation process, the leitmotif of his earlier writings. In volume 2 of the *Treatise*, devoted to applied monetary theory, Keynes makes this conceptualization particularly luminous, especially by quoting historical illustrations in support of his argument. The wealth of the world, Keynes argued, was made possible by the sacrifices of whole generations in foregoing present consumption in the hope of a higher standard of consumption in the future. It is wrong, however, to think that abstinence alone was enough to generate an augmentation in a country's material wealth. As is clear from the first fundamental equation, savings, if unaccompanied by an adequate flow of investment, will merely provoke a fall in prices, entailing a transfer of purchasing power from one set of consumers to another.

---

7. "Alfred Marshall 1842–1924," *The Economic Journal*, September 1924; reprinted in *C.W.K.* 10:196.

The vital cog in the accumulation mechanism is thus investment, which is the fruit of the entrepreneurial spirit, and its driving force is the expectation of profit. Historical experience of the development process in Spain, France, and Britain during the sixteenth and seventeenth centuries shows that the most rapid leaps toward a capitalist structure, or the periods of most intensive economic activity and real accumulation, occurred when prices outpaced wages, and thus when realized and expected profits were increasing.[8] On the other hand, as more recent experience made even more evident, periods of stagnation or income and wealth regression were marked in periods in which profits had fallen.

In terms of the fundamental equations of the *Treatise*, the capitalist system's cyclical phases could be interpreted as entailing a natural rate of interest which is respectively rising or falling and in which, for reasons linked to the structure and behavior of financial institutions, the market rate lags in adapting to the real rate. Oscillations in the price level accompanied crises inevitably linked to an imbalance between investment and savings. Inasmuch as savings habits remained relatively stable over time the real causes of crises were variations in the expected return on investment unmatched by an equally rapid adaptation in the cost of finance. Crises attributed to an excess of investment fever over savings were favorable to accumulation. Generally these periods were a product of low real wages, or a forced cramping of real consumption via inflation. It is true that even voluntary saving implies, by definition, deferred consumption. "Forced saving" via inflation redistributes wealth from labor to profits.[9] To minimize the unsavory aspect of this real wage erosion meant a commitment to the hypothesis that a continuous accumulation of wealth was an unassailable objective.

Keynes's conclusion was consistent with the analysis of the *Treatise* (volume 1) and many of his earlier writings. He believed that monetary policy should by all means avoid crises due to excess

8. Keynes referred to the studies of E. J. Hamilton, presented in 1928–29, on the ramifications of the flow of gold to Europe following the discovery of America.

9. Modern writers seldom refer to "forced savings." The concept has practically disappeared from the lexicon, yet it was prominent in the literature of the 1930s, in Keynes, Robertson, Hayek, Von Mises; but much earlier it may be found in Robert Malthus, *Principles of Political Economy* (1820; reprint, Oxford: Basil Blackwell, A. M. Kelly, 1951).

savings, and that the policy aim should be to balance out savings and investment. Meanwhile, investment decisions ought to be relieved of exclusive dependence on ephemeral circumstance:

> Nevertheless I am not yet converted, taking everything into account, from a preference for a policy today which, whilst avoiding deflation at all costs, aims at the stability of purchasing power as its ideal objective. Perhaps the ultimate solution lies in the rate of capital development becoming more largely an affair of state, determined by collective wisdom and long views. If the task of accumulation comes to depend somewhat less on individual caprice, so as to be no longer at the mercy of calculations partly based on the expectation of life of the particular mortal men who are alive today, the dilemma between thrift and profits as the means of securing the most desirable rate of growth for the community's aggregate wealth will cease to present itself.[10]

Keynes's vision that investment might gradually free itself from the vacillations of unstable subjective expectations exposes an intuition which was to be important in the future development of his thinking. Nonetheless, it also reveals the significance of certain important gaps in his analysis. In the *Treatise* the theory of crisis devolves from a sequence in which a profit interval is followed by a period of losses. The former has a positive, the latter a negative impact on investment. Recalling, however, that Keynes defines these sums as the discrepancy between receipts and costs, where costs include "interest on capital" and "a normal remuneration to the entrepreneur," it is clear that the only way in which profits and losses can be associated with an imbalance between savings and investment is by relying on a theory of the "normal" rate of profit based precisely on these two cost items.

A proper theory should explain the long-term trend in the "normal" profit rate as capital accumulates, making it possible thereby to identify deviations from the trend as being due to the pressure of cyclical forces. Here, the analytical weakness of Keynes, as compared to the classicists' theory, is particularly pronounced. Ricardo and Marx offer an explanation integrating accumulation and growth with the rate of profit and "normal" prices. Although these explanations suffer from their own limitations they provide a logical

---

10. *Treatise*, in *C.W.K.* 6:145.

framework (as Marx used it) to explain crises. All that is necessary is to recognize, as Keynes did, the existence of insufficient demand. Keynes, however, who had apparently adopted his concepts of "interest on capital" and "normal remuneration to the entrepreneur" from Marshall, was completely unable to forge an analytical tie between accumulation and economic crisis.

Even here, however, the blockage did not dispose Keynes to conceal the problem of having to take a clear stand vis-à-vis the classicists' view that capital accumulation and growth would gradually urge the rate of profit down.

It is important to set out clearly Keynes's position on this point. Otherwise his concern with establishing conditions capable of insuring a regular and continuous flow of investment, and the recommendations to this end which appear in the *Treatise*, and even more often in the *General Theory*, would appear superfluous or even schizophrenic. The only justification for his prescriptive concern was, in fact, his great faith that so long as capital continued to accumulate the return on capital would be sufficient to propel further accumulation. This faith ensued from a profound conviction that technical progress, and the institutional transformation of society, would strengthen the return on capital sufficiently to reverse the opposite drift associated with the purely quantitative growth in capital itself.

An echo of this conviction pokes up in certain passages of *Economic Possibilities for Our Grand Children*, a short essay prepared for a conference (in 1928) and published two years later.[11] Despite the traumatic crisis of the world economy at the time, the tone of the essay reflected an easy optimism about the economic future. Keynes foresaw that, within a hundred years, the economic problem, which had always been the "most pressing problem for the human race," would no longer be the dismal imperative. He based this forecast on a simple extrapolation of the results achieved, in just a few generations, by the industrialized countries of Europe and America, thanks to the conjunction of technological innovation and capital accumulation:

> If capital increases, say, 2 per cent per annum, the capital equipment of the world will have increased by a half in twenty years, and

---

11. Reprinted in *C.W.K.*, vol. 9.

seven and a half times in a hundred years. Think of this in terms of material things—houses, transport, and the like.

At the same time technical improvements in manufacture and transport have been proceeding at a greater rate in the last ten years than ever before in history. . . . There is evidence that the revolutionary technical changes, which have so far chiefly affected industry, may soon be attacking agriculture.

. . . In quite a few years—in our own lifetime I mean—we may be able to perform all the operations of agriculture, mining, and manufacture with a quarter of the human effort to which we have been accustomed. (P. 325)

Keynes did not ignore the fact that the transition to more capital intensive techniques of production could be so rapid as to cause strains in absorbing labor. But these would be purely temporary, nothing more than a disruptive period of settling in toward a definitive equilibrium:

For the moment the very rapidity of these changes is hurting us and bringing difficult problems to solve. Those countries are suffering relatively which are not in the vanguard of progress. We are being afflicted with a new disease of which some readers may not yet have heard the name, but of which they will hear a great deal in the years to come—namely, *technological unemployment*. This means unemployment due to our discovery of means of economising the use of labour outrunning the pace at which we can find new uses for labour. But this is only a temporary phase of maladjustment. All this means in the long run *that mankind is solving its economic problems*. (P. 325)

This idea that after a period of sustained intense growth the economic system could resolve the cruel mismatch between the scarcity of resources and reasonable consumption needs constituted a spectacular break between Keynes's vision of capitalism and the black picture of the classicists, especially Marx, who foresaw the stimulation of new needs as the very essence of the capitalist system. New needs engendered new investment opportunities in an inexorable growth evolution in which capital accumulation could not be impeded without inflicting a breakdown in the very structure of the system. In this view the only threat to incessant accumulation was the fall in the rate of profit due, according to Ricardo, to the scarcity of primary factors and, according to Marx, to increasing capital intensity which leads to discarding workers to the scrapheap of the industrial labor-reserve army.[12] For Keynes, the decline in the rate of profit was not a menace. When it appeared, it would mean that capitalism had achieved a "paradise on earth."

The great crisis of the thirties led him to reflect more deeply on this point. The position on the future of capitalism expressed in the *General Theory* is more cautious.

Given the "state of the art" of the late 1920s, what were the innovations introduced by the *Treatise* specifically in the field of monetary theory? It is this question, posed initially, which now deserves attention.

Neoclassical theory visualizes the essential role of money as a circulatory means of exchange. Although its role as a store of value was not excluded at a conceptual level, it is analytically irrelevant in the conception of equilibrium. In the most rigorous analytical formulation of the theory, as in Leon Walras, money is nothing more than the standard giving numerical dimension to the absolute price level.[13] Hence the equation of the quantity theory could be merely superimposed on the system of equations worked up to determine relative barter-economy prices. Thus, by stipulating a given quantity of money and its velocity of circulation, one could calculate the general price level compatible with a given volume of transactions, that is, with the physical quantities of different goods produced.[14] Theoretically, the most important consequence of this analytical device is that changes in the quantity of money leave relative prices undisturbed;[15] the practically significant point is the conviction that

12. For a reflection on this theme see J. Robinson, *Freedom and Necessity* (London: Allen and Unwin, 1970).

13. *Elements d'economie politique pure* (Paris, 1926); translated under the title *Elements of Pure Economics* (London: Allen and Unwin, 1954).

14. For a recent clear analysis in depth of the role of money in Walras's general equilibrium, see M. Morishima, "Leon Walras and Money," in *Current Economic Problems*, ed. M. Makin and A. R. Nobay (Cambridge: At the University Press, 1975).

15. More recently, during the period between the end of the 1940s and the beginning of the 1960s, the logical foundations for this dichotomy between the way the neoclassical model determines absolute and relative prices have been at the center of a heated debate presented by F. Modigliani, "The Monetary Mechanism and Its Interreaction with Real Phenomena," *The Review of Economics and Statistics* (February 1963), and D. Patinkin, *Money, Interest and Prices* (New York: Harper and Row, 1965); see also the broad-ranging bibliography in the latter work.

the purchasing power of money is "neutral" with respect to real economic magnitudes.

Wicksell's monetary theory occupies a special niche in the neoclassical wisdom. In *Geldzins und Güterpreise*, published in 1898, Wicksell recognizes the importance of upheavals in the general price level in a world in which many economic magnitudes are rigid in monetary terms, alluding implicitly to the redistributive burdens that these may engender.[16] Yet in his subsequent analysis, he withdraws from the inherent consequences. Nonetheless, Wicksell does note the quandary innate to the mechanism whereby variations in the money quantity perturb the general price level. His solution, based on the difference between the rate of interest charged by the banks and "the natural rate of interest on capital" is original; it marks for the first time that the nexus between money and prices is explicitly attached to the effect of the interest rate on investment.

Wicksell defines the natural rate of interest as "the rate of interest which would be determined by supply and demand if no use were made of money and all lending were effected in the form of real capital goods."[17] The determination emanates from a theory of capital which recent criticism has revealed as subject to serious theoretical deficiencies.[18] Nonetheless, Wicksell undisputably occupies a distinguished position in that his theory was easily the most advanced of the monetary perceptions of the neoclassical standard bearers.

The analogy between the central body of Wicksell's analysis and the line followed by the *Treatise* renders suspect the originality—or priority—of Keynes's thinking, despite its independence in conception. Actually the content of the theory of investment in the *Treatise* or its descendant in the *General Theory*, and Wicksell's theory of capital, are very different.[19] In any case, while Keynes

---

16. (Jena: G. Fisher, 1898); translated under the title *Interest and Prices* (London: Macmillan, 1936), chap. 1.

17. Ibid., p. 102.

18. See P. Garegnani, *Il capitale nelle teorie della distribuzione* (Milan: Giuffrè, 1960).

19. It is also apparent that Wicksell's critique of the quantity theory of money is much less advanced than Keynes's. The only sources of velocity variations elicited by Wicksell stem from different institutional forms of organization of money and credit. This warrants Keynes's judgment that "Wicksell's theory is closely akin to the theory of this treatise, though he

notes the similarity between his own "credit cycle" theory and that provided by Wicksell, he commented in the *Treatise* that his command of the German language was so poor it prevented any grasp of anything he did not already know![20] Bearing this in mind, and the fact that the English translation of *Geldzins und Güterpreise* appeared in 1936,[21] it is quite certain that despite strands of similarity the two formulations were the fruit of completely independent origins.

Keynes's debt to Marshall's monetary thinking had already been elaborated in the context of *A Tract on Monetary Reform*. Keynes had been stimulated to plunge deeper into the causal mechanisms implicit in the quantity theory by his earlier immersion conceptions elaborated by Marshall during his teaching at Cambridge.

Keynes noted with regret that Marshall's procrastination in publishing his monetary writings had blocked earlier discussion of many original hints begging development. Prior to the 1923 publication of *Money, Credit and Commerce*,[22] Marshall's monetary thinking had been spread only by oral tradition through several disciples. As a result, the only available presentation of one of the most intriguing aspects of his monetary theory—the ancient and still modern transmission channel through which money affects prices—was contained in his evidence to the Gold and Silver Commission in 1887 and to the Indian Currency Committee in 1899. "It was an odd state of affairs," Keynes concluded, "that one of the most fundamental parts of Monetary Theory should, for about a quarter of century, have been available to students nowhere except embedded in the form of question—and—answer before a Government Commission interested in a transitory practical problem."[23]

To Keynes, Marshall had made a profound impact on monetary theory. Among Marshall's theses was the determination of the value of money by the equilibrium between demand and supply,

---

was not successful, in my opinion, in linking up his theory of bank rate to the quantity equation" (*Treatise*, in *C.W.K.* 5:167).

20. "In German I can only clearly understand what I know already!—so that *new* ideas are apt to be veiled from me by the difficulties of language" (ibid., p. 178 n. 2).

21. By Richard Kahn, and one suspects, at Keynes's direct or indirect instigation.

22. London: Macmillan.

23. "Alfred Marshall," in *C.W.K.* 10:192.

expressed in terms of the purchasing power which people wished to hold in liquid form compared to the quantity of money supplied by the monetary system: the individual decision criteria included the importance attached to the liquid money asset compared to the interest-yielding (and speculative) advantages promised by other ways of holding wealth. There was also the distinction between the *real* and the *money* rate of interest, which Keynes clearly perceived in the first edition of the *Principles of Economics* (1890) prior to its appearance in Irving Fisher's book. Also elaborated was the purchasing power parity theory (originating more implicitly in Hume and then in Ricardo), and normally attributed to Gustav Cassel but certainly clearly enunciated by Marshall in his evidence to the Gold and Silver Commission.[24]

This fealty by Keynes seems like ample proof of his perception of the continuity of his thought as in a linear progression from Marshall. If one considers the significance for Keynesian liquidity theory of Marshall's supply and demand approach to money, and his analysis of the advantages at the margin of holding money rather than other forms of wealth, the conclusion is reinforced. Nonetheless, the *Treatise* also shows a certain disgruntlement with Marshall's interpretation of the causal chain between money augmentation and the reaction in prices, explained in terms of incentives for speculation ensuing from downward pressures in the rate of interest. The logic of speculation depends on the margin separating the expected rate of inflation and the cost of money. To concentrate attention exclusively or predominantly on this phenomenon would imply that the money supply increase would have an immediate inflationary "announcement" effect. Here one would still have to explain why this "shock" effect actually occurs.

To attribute the inflationary expectation to mere chance, or to errors of forecasting, is intellectually incomplete. Keynes thus has to feel his way without help from his mentor:

> This seems to me to be the doctrine on which I was brought up, and which certainly did not bring home to my mind any clear idea of the relationship between the volume of earnings at any time, the volume of savings, and the volume of goods coming forward available for

---

24. Ibid., pp. 191–95.

consumption, or of the connection of these things with the equilibrium between savings and investment.[25]

Among Keynes's contemporaries the heresy of the *Treatise* was shared, at least in part, by Ralph G. Hawtrey and Dennis H. Robertson.[26] In the *Treatise* (vol. 1) Keynes praised the economist who, in his view, had come closest to his own conception of the role of the rate of interest in monetary theory. He recognized Hawtrey's merit in having isolated the channel through which money can influence prices, that is, through the rate of interest affecting investment. His criticism of Hawtrey centered on the latter's targeting of one particular kind of investment, namely, stocks of inventories which sellers hold as a cushion allowing them to cover sales orders without interruption.

To Keynes, inventory investment stocks were not particularly sensitive to interest rate fluctuations; there was not the slightest reason to believe that a higher cost of money would exert a greater influence on the behavior of sellers in the marketing network than on producers.

The critical tone, however, was very bland. Keynes was really reproaching a colleague searching for the light for his failure to carry a correct and original line of analysis to its logical conclusions. Relations between the two economists were cordial, and their views overlapped so much that Keynes sent Hawtrey the first proofs of the *Treatise* in the spring and summer of 1930. In truth, Keynes sent Hawtrey the pages not only to benefit from outside criticism (Hawtrey was a Treasury official rather than an academic) but also to persuade him of the validity of his arguments on a number of points under review in a study commission which Philip Snowden, the chancellor of the Exchequer, had set up in 1929. Keynes concluded his covering letter: "I wonder if I shall convince you! Because, although we always seem to differ on these monetary questions in discussion, I feel that ultimately I am joined in common agreement with you as against most of the rest of the world."[27]

Keynes's personal relations and collaboration with Dennis

---

25. *Treatise*, in *C.W.K.* 5:172–73.

26. For certain points in common between Keynes's thinking and that of his contemporaries see the brilliant study by F. Caffè, "Keynes e i suoi contemporanei," *Note Economiche*, September–December 1975.

27. *C.W.K.* 13:132.

Robertson were even closer. (Robertson signed his correspondence with Keynes himself, "your affectionate pupil.") In *Banking Policy and the Price Level*, which Robertson had published in 1926, Keynes felt keenly "my indebtedness for clues which have set my mind working in the right direction."[28]

Naturally enough, Robertson had a number of criticisms of the *Treatise*, and Keynes replied point by point, provoking a debate in the pages of the *Economic Journal* and in a voluminous correspondence lasting over two years, from 1931 to 1933.

Some of the points of contention went to detail and terminology; others were judgmental, and still others dwelt on fundamental theoretical disagreements. One point in particular seems symptomatic of the hurdles inherent in one aspect of Keynes's monetary theory—the equilibrium in the stock of financial assets—vis-à-vis the traditional theory.

Robertson faulted the mechanism whereby Keynes used his fundamental equations to explain price perturbations.[29] The only circumstances, Robertson argues, in which an excess of savings (S) over investment (I') could reduce the price level for consumer goods (P) without altering the price level for investment goods (P') would be if the savings excess were hoarded. Conversely, if the excess savings were translated into an increased demand for shares (equities), rather than for liquid reserves, then the price of shares, and thus P', would tend to edge up. This would create a situation in which investment (I) could once again balance the increased flow of savings (S). Again $S - I = 0$, even when the cost of investment is below total savings, that is, when $(S - I') > 0$. As a result of all this, on the basis of the second fundamental equation the general price level (Π) would hold firm while the fall in P would be counterbalanced by an uptick in P'. This criticism implies an interpretation of the link between real and financial flows completely extraneous to the *Treatise* approach based on the equilibrium between the demand and supply of stocks of different financial assets. Keynes in his reply to Robertson observed that the increased demand for financial assets (created by excess savings) is balanced by an in-

---

28. *Treatise*, in *C.W.K.* 5:154 n. 1.

29. "Mr. Keynes' Theory of Money," *The Economic Journal*, September 1931.

creased supply through losses sustained in the consumer goods sector.[30] The latter producers, in order to cover their losses, are forced to drain their financial reserves, selling shares and money. Price P' will tend to change only when savers' financial preferences are unaligned with those of producers, though there is no reason to suppose that this actually happens:

> Unless the propensity to hoard of the savers is different from the propensity to hoard of the entrepreneurs—and if it is different, it will mean that there is a change of hoarding-propensity for the community as a whole, which change is as likely à priori to be in one direction as in the other—it follows that the excess of saving has in itself, and apart from its repercussions on the aggregate propensity to hoard, no tendency to cause any change at all in the price of non-liquid assets.[31]

The sense of Keynes's reply is that P' is determined by the equilibrium between the desired composition of financial assets, as shown by savers' preference schedules, and the composition of the supply of financial liabilities, reflected in the preference schedules of banks and producers. As Keynes supposes savers and producers to have the same propensity to hoard with respect to a given positive or negative wealth flow, he was saying that the equilibrium rate of return is uniquely determined by the composition of the existing stock of financial assets.

The frontal attack against the *Treatise*'s analytical apparatus however was orchestrated by Friedrich A. von Hayek,[32] who, along with Ludwig von Mises and Hans Neisser, was an authoritative spokesman for the new Austrian monetary school. Keynes had defined this school as "neo-Wicksellian" and had recognized its priority in pinning the trade cycles on the relation between the interest rate and the equilibrium between savings and investment, that is, a structure paralleling the *Treatise*.

Hayek's review was highly detailed, though centered mainly

---

30. "Rejoinder," *The Economic Journal*, September 1931.

31. Ibid., p. 415.

32. Hayek, "Reflections on the Pure Theory of Money of Mr. J. M. Keynes," *Economica*, August 1931.

on two main themes. The first of these concerned the micro-foundation of the *Treatise*'s aggregate analysis. According to Hayek, the basis was nonexistent, or at any rate far from explicit. This explained Keynes's failure to determine precisely his concepts of profit and investment, and the inacceptability of an unequivocal relationship between profit and the demand for factors of production. Hayek's point of reference was the theory of production and capital developed by E. von Böhm-Bawerk,[33] and it is in this context that he assessed Keynes's propositions concerning profit and investment. Referring back to Böhm-Bawerk's approach, based on the different stages in the productive process, Hayek hypothesizes a situation in which firms in the consumer goods sector engaged in the production of intermediate goods suffer from a production surfeit, while firms closer to the final stage experience a situation of excess demand. Here, the losses suffered by the former may compensate for the profits of the latter. Keynes's own definitions thus lead to the conclusion that the profit of the whole sector is zero. At the same time, however, there may be a change in the total demand for original factors of production, for profitable firms will limit themselves to using a higher volume of intermediate products, whereas losing firms will lay off workers. It follows that there is no necessary link between factor demand and the presence of profits or losses.

As far as investment is concerned, Hayek argues that it is impossible to calculate the return on the production of capital goods without first having a "complete theory of capital." The decision whether to produce consumer or investment goods is not an arbitrary one. The only way to measure the influence of "changes in technical knowledge and the relative demand for different consumption goods" (p. 285) on comparative profits is to start from a theory of capital. For Hayek, who rigidly stuck to Böhm-Bawerk's theory of the "average period of production," the idea of a clear distinction between the production of capital goods and that of consumer goods was "misleading." *"The alternative,"* he wrote, *"is not between producing consumption or investment goods, but between producing investment goods which will yield consumption goods at a more or less distant date in the future"* (p. 286).

---

33. Böhm-Bawerk, *Positive Theory of Capital* (London: Macmillan, 1891).

It is strange, he insisted, that Keynes should compare his theory to Wicksell's while he "ignores completely the general theoretical basis of Wicksell's theory." Even more surprising is that Keynes should rediscover certain aspects of Böhm-Bawerk's capital theory without immersing himself in the central body of the theory.[34]

The other theme on which Hayek lavishes his criticism is the relationship between the quantity of money and the savings-investment gap. To Hayek an excess of investment over savings is only possible when the credit granted by the banking system outruns savings. Thus "any change in the circulation *must* be accompanied by a divergence between savings and investment" (pp. 292–93). There is thus no point in Keynes's distinction between an increase in the demand for money due to a rise in the unit cost of production (W_1) and a variation in circulation aimed at opening a gap between savings and investment. The distinction between variations in prices along the equilibrium path where prices and costs are equal, and disturbances due to excess of savings or investment, is similarly devoid of analytical significance. As far as monetary policy is concerned, it is impossible to manipulate money without perturbing the delicate savings and investment equilibrium. It thus follows—and this is the main theme of Hayek's monetary theory expressed in his key work *Prices and Production*[35]—that monetary policy should be "neutral": to equate the supply of credit to savings, the quantity of money should be held constant.

Keynes in his reply refers back to *Prices and Production* on the presumption that Hayek's critique of the *Treatise* is a natural derivative.[36] When Hayek claims that when "more (or less) money is being invested than is being saved is equivalent to so much money being added to (or withdrawn from) industrial circulation, so that the total of profits, or the difference between the expenditure and the receipts of the entrepreneurs, which is the essential element in the second term of the fundamental equations, will be equal to the net addition to (or subtraction from) the effective circulation," he is

---

34. Hayek is alluding to the formula presented in Keynes, *Treatise*, in *C.W.K.*, vol. 5, chap. 20.

35. London: G. Routledge and Sons, 1931.

36. "The Pure Theory of Money: A Reply to Dr. Hayek," *Economica*, November 1931.

attributing to Keynes a line of analysis completely extraneous to the *Treatise*.[37]

To get to the bottom of this erroneous interpretation of the fundamental equations it was necessary, Keynes thought, to consider Hayek's general theoretical approach in *Prices and Production*, where "voluntary" savings are automatically translated into investment. Supposing that all savings are held as bank deposits, and that the banking system grants a volume of credit outrunning original deposits, this will create additional investment and "forced" savings. Thus, if the banks recycle the same quantity of money as they receive or avoid the creation of new money, then the demand and supply of real capital will be in harmony.

Keynes saw no logical basis for this simple correlation between variations in money and the investment flow. The additional money obtained by entrepreneurs may be used either to offset their losses or to purchase capital goods. At the same time, if a citizen decides to sell bonds to a bank, and the latter decides not to neutralize the operation but to allow an increase in the volume of its deposits, the result is more money without any direct effect on either savings or investment. The idea that more money immediately augments purchasing power spent on capital goods is undoubtedly akin to the traditional quantity theory, and if this was the gist of the *Treatise*, the orthodox link would be apparent. But this was not the case. In the *Treatise*, savings and investment could diverge, regardless of whether or not the banking system abandons a policy of "neutrality": "merely as a result of the public changing their rate of saving or the entrepreneurs changing their rate of investment, there being no automatic mechanism in the economic system (as Dr. Hayek's view would imply there must be) to keep the two rates equal, provided that the effective quantity of money is unchanged."[38]

This independent behavior of real flows regardless of monetary factors makes any contact with the quantity theory harder; in fact, it implies a radical break with traditional theory. The switch from the old to the new theoretical view can be painful: "Thus those who are sufficiently steeped in the old point of view simply cannot

37. Hayek, "Reflections," pp. 290–91; and Keynes, "The Pure Theory of Money," pp. 387–88.
38. "The Pure Theory of Money," p. 393.

bring themselves to believe that I am asking them to step into a new pair of trousers, and will insist on regarding it as nothing but an embroidered version of the old pair which they have been wearing for years."[39]

For Keynes then, Hayek's expression of Böhm-Bawerk was a refined version of that dominant traditional theory which he was later, in the *General Theory*, to denigrate as the "classical" theory. He attributed the hypothesis that investment adapts mechanically so as to match savings to this tradition, a hypothesis always above or below the surface in Hayek's reasoning. Keynes's rejection, his disdain for the "classical economics" balancing act of savings and investment, did not dismiss the mechanism whereby the two flows converged via the rate of interest. This mechanism was espoused by the Keynes of the *Treatise*. Keynes's rejection concerned the idea that an expansion of bank credit to surpass savings is a necessary and sufficient condition to allow an equal investment excess. Underlying this concept there is the conviction (inherent in Say's Law) that every pound of income not spent on consumption is constantly destined for investment. This is tantamount to insisting that investment is not a behavioral function but a variable molded to the volume of "voluntary savings" and the issuance of new money. As the *Treatise* entrusted the market rate of interest as the balancing agent for flows of savings and investment, each emanating from distinct and independent decisions, it lies outside the domain of the venerable tradition.

As far as Hayek's insistence on Keynes's lack of a theory of capital is concerned, Keynes readily conceded that its inclusion in the *Treatise* would have enabled him to build his monetary analysis on firmer foundations. But he also remarked that there was no satisfactory theory of capital:

> Dr. Hayek complains that I do not myself propound any satisfactory theory of capital and interest and that I do not build on any existing theory. He means by this, I take it, the theory of capital accumulation relatively to the rate of consumption and the factors which determine the natural rate of interest. This is quite true; and I agree with Dr. Hayek that a development of this theory would be highly relevant to my treatment of monetary matters and likely to throw light into dark corners. It is very possible that, looking back after a

39. Ibid., p. 390.

satisfactory theory has been completed, we shall see that the ideas
which Böhm-Bawerk was driving at, lie at the heart of the problem
and that the neglect of him by English pre-war economists was as
mistaken as their neglect of Wicksell. But there is no such theory at
present, and, as Dr. Hayek would agree, a thorough treatment of it
might lead one rather a long way from monetary theory.[40]

The Keynes-Hayek controversy remains of decided theoretical importance, with a significance beyond the specific points raised
during the debate. Hayek professed that an ideal monetary policy
should be "neutral." By holding the quantity of money (or more
precisely *MV*, which includes the velocity) constant, money would
inflict no monetary disorder on the crucial real variables of the system. The idea was tied to the concepts of monetary policy alive—
and still afloat—during the 1920s and which were the target for
much of the spirited analysis in *A Tract on Monetary Reform*. In
Hayek, as in the new Austrian monetary school generally, the monetary policy response to the crises of the late 1920s did not invali-
date the conventional programs of the traditional theory. Instead,
there had only been an advance in the analytical foundations of the
venerable prescriptions.

To refute the Austrian School's policy implications it was
therefore necessary to refute their conceptual foundations. Keynes,
as we have seen, concentrated his fire on the savings and investment equilibrium. Almost simultaneously, in a review of *Prices and
Production*, Piero Sraffa published a thorough-going critique which
laid bare Hayek's whole conception of money (and monetary policy)
as resting on the postulate that the real or nonmonetary system was
intrinsically stable.[41]

Hayek's commendable aim, Sraffa observes, was to study the
impact of variations in the quantity of money on relative prices. En
route, however, he lost sight of his original intention, concentrating
instead on the monetary maneuver necessary to bind savings and
investment decisions as effectively as if they occurred in a barter
economy. Hayek treats money exclusively as a medium of exchange, neglecting the existence of contracts fixed in monetary terms
and thus denying any importance to the notion of variations in the
general price level. He reaches the conclusion that the only "neu-

40. Ibid., p. 394.
41. "Dr. Hayek on Money and Capital," *The Economic Journal*, March
1932.

tral" monetary policy—the only policy that would not disturb the individual decisions typical of a nonmonetary economy—is a policy that maintains the quantity of money constant. This conclusion, as it emerged from the controversy with Keynes, was bound up to the idea that any money augmentation would generate a volume of investment in excess of savings, implying a demand excess in consumer goods whose prices would thus increase and induce a neutralizing volume of "forced" savings. Unlike "voluntary" savings, however, "forced" accumulation is an unstable process. The increase in investment will in fact push up wages and incomes in the capital goods sector, allowing consumers to claim back the capital filched from them. This increase in production costs thereupon rapidly absorbs the additional bank money injected into the system, making it impossible for entrepreneurs to sustain the higher rate of accumulation, and even preventing them from maintaining their capital plant. The inevitable depreciation of existing capital, interpreted as a consumption of capital, moves the system to a return to the level of capital intensity prevailing prior to the money increase.

In a rejoinder to a reply by Hayek, Sraffa had no difficulty in showing that on Hayek's own hypothesis concerning the proportionality between the increase in the quantity of money, the increase in capital, the increase in the number of stages in the productive process, and the increase in the volume of transactions, there was absolutely no logic to his distinction between voluntary and forced accumulation. Hayek's hypothesis precluded any increase in monetary incomes in the capital goods sector, as the increase in money would be entirely absorbed by the increased demand for liquid reserves.

Quite apart from this point, however, Sraffa sought to identify the innate reason for Hayek's fear of money as the main internal threat to systemic stability. According to Hayek: "In a money economy, the actual or money rate of interest may differ from the equilibrium or natural rate, because the demand for and the supply of capital do not meet in their natural form but in the form of money, the quantity of which available for capital purposes may be arbitrarily changed by banks."[42]

This proposition, together with the peremptory statement that

---

42. Hayek, *Prices and Production*, pp. 20–21; and Sraffa, "Money and Capital: A Rejoinder," *The Economic Journal* (June 1932), p. 49.

the volume of credit granted by the banks should exactly dovetail with savings, grinds on to the logical conclusion that Wicksell's "natural" rate of interest—which Hayek reduces to a simple "equilibrium" rate—corresponds to the money rate when the flow of credit is regulated in such a way as to exactly conform to the flow of savings. If the banks grant more credit, the money interest rate drops. Nevertheless, as the increase in credit underwrites an identical additional volume of investment, the new money rate no longer preserves the savings and investment equilibrium. In a nonmonetary economy, where loans are made *in natura*, and the interest rate is expressed in terms of goods, this kind of disequilibrium is precluded. An ideal policy in a monetary economy is thus one that replicates the situation in an economy where money does not exist. This implies that the quantity of money in circulation should be held constant (attaching a constancy also to velocity—by assumption).

The reasoning would be logically impeccable if the equilibrium of the underlying nonmonetary system were intrinsically stable. This implies equality between rates of interest expressed in terms of different goods; otherwise it would be illegitimate to attribute disequilibria to monetary factors alone.

Sraffa observed that the rate of interest on loans in terms of goods ("commodity rate") is influenced by the disparity between current and expected prices. Expected prices for each good depend, in turn, on current imbalances between demand and supply; excess current demand drives prices up above the equilibrium level, igniting expectations of a future fall. The opposite applies to an excess of supply.

Thus to maintain a single equilibrium rate of interest in a nonmonetary barter economy entails the absence of excess supply or demand for any single good, or a freedom from pressure of any kind capable of forcing a gap between current and expected prices. In an economy characterized by capital accumulation, such as that sketched by Hayek, the normal position would be very different because of incessant shifts of demand—and the ensuing production—from good to good. In these circumstances, a nonmonetary economy would not have merely one "natural" rate of interest but many—one for each good. Sraffa thus queries the sense of comparing this open band of rates with the market rate for credit formed in a monetary economy. Wicksell conceived of a "natural" rate as being calculated as the average rate for individual goods, weighted by their contribution to the general price level, thereby averting this stumbling block.[43] Hayek, however, had rejected right at the start of his analysis the concept of an "average," or even that of price level, precluding the strained Wicksell resolution.

The conclusion to be drawn from Sraffa's powerful critique is that the stability of a nonmonetary economy is not inherent in the "nature of things," but rather it has to be assumed a priori by invoking the hypothesis that supply and demand for each individual good are in equilibrium. This is the only (totally unrealistic) hypothesis by which crises can be attributed to a money economy that are barred to barter economies.

This conclusion is substantially the same as that reached by Keynes in his reply to Hayek. Keynes's macroeconomic defense of the *Treatise* was coherent in his rejection of any mechanical and a priori equivalence between savings and investment. On the microeconomic terrain chosen by Hayek for his attack, Sraffa's analysis was however more powerful. Keynes was to return to it in his *General Theory*.

---

43. Sraffa shied away from the Wicksell concoction because the "natural" rate of interest then depended on an arbitrary undetermined choice of the composite commodity entered as a unit of measurement for the price level.

CHAPTER 7

THE LOGICAL PREMISE
TO A CRITIQUE
OF THE TRADITIONAL THEORY

Keynes's reply to Hayek, and Sraffa's intervention in the debate, struck a decisive blow at the inchoate, ubiquitous, and never completely defeated idea of a "neutral" monetary policy as some kind of optimum. The discussion, furthermore, clarified the central role of investment theory in the relationship between money, prices, and crises. Mindful of Keynes's admirable willingness to reexamine his own notions, it is reasonable to surmise that his debate with the Austrian monetary school encouraged him to reflect further on investment, as presented in the *Treatise*. Other factors were urging him in the same direction: there were the critical observations formulated by the group of young economists belonging to the Cambridge "Circus" and, more poignantly, the gravity of domestic and international economic events at the onset of the 1930s.

During the first half of 1931 a number of young Cambridge economists debated the content and significance of the *Treatise*; one criticism that emerged was directly concerned with investment: in correspondence Richard Kahn, a pupil of Keynes's, took exception to the *Treatise*'s explanation of the theory of prices for capital goods. Kahn noted an unjustified asymmetry between the price level theory for consumer goods (P), and that for capital goods (P'): the price level for consumer goods was said to be determined by demand and supply, while the price level for investment goods was attributed to "external" causes such as savers' financial preferences and the operations of the banking system, and was thus considered to be subject to speculative eruptions inherent within the system. "If the price level of consumption goods is rigidly determined by the difference between savings and cost of investment, why—asks Kahn—is not the price level of investment goods equally rigidly determined by the difference between expenditure on consumption goods and the cost of producing consumption goods?"[1]

The only possible warrant for this asymmetry is "the fact that there exists no demand curve for consumption goods on the part of the speculators" or the fact that if this demand does exist "it is relatively inelastic." But then, as Joan Robinson also agreed,[2] the discrepancy between the two processes could be only "of degree and not an absolute one in logic."[3]

Put in these terms the divergency would mainly consist of different hypotheses about supply elasticities; the excess demand or supply in the capital goods sector creates prices expectations that are conducive to variations in stocks (out of inventory) capable of erasing the excess, and thus maintaining the current price level unaltered. For consumer goods, perishability and smaller inventories compared to the production flow make it impossible to bridge the gap between current supply and demand so that the unbalance is reflected in the price level. Now if savings were considered as "demand" for investment goods, the diverse mechanism for determining the two price levels would be logically sustainable and the theoretical disparity would be more apparent than real. Taking total income as divided between consumption and savings, and total output as the sum of the combined output of consumption and investment goods, the identity of income and output (at cost value) would imply that an excess of demand for investment goods would generate an equal and opposite excess in the consumer goods sector. This would explain the contrasting pressures on the two price levels detected by Kahn, and the hypotheses resting on inventories as a brake on these pressures.

Keynes had, however, long ceased to consider savings as automatic demand for investment. It was futile, therefore, to expect him to ferret out a symmetry between reciprocal excesses of demand and supply in the two sectors and to underscore them in the fundamental equations of the *Treatise*. The study of the effects of interest rates on investment (volume 1, chapter 13) was based on the hypothesis that production and demand for capital goods are

---

1. *C.W.K.* 13:203.

2. Robinson, "A Parable on Saving and Investment," *Economica*, February 1933.

3. *C.W.K.* 13:219.

continually being aligned. A less casual examination would reveal, however, that this supply and demand equality would be achieved in the most trivial way, ensuing from decisions taken to order investment goods and a demand capability for absorbing any level of production—and always at a uniform price. Consider this passage:

> Now, from the point view of individual entrepreneurs, there will be no occasion for a reduction in the output of such goods, unless their price is falling relatively to their cost of production, or unless the demand for them is falling off at the existing price. In what way can a rise in bank rate tend to bring this about?
>
> Upon what does the demand price of capital goods depend? It depends on *two* things—on estimated net prospective yield from fixed capital (estimated by the opinion of the market after such allowance as they choose to make for the uncertainty of anticipation, etc.), measured in money, and on the rate of interest at which this future yield is capitalised. It follows that the price of such goods can change for either of two reasons—because the prospective yield has changed or because the rate of interest has changed.[4]

The underlying logic of this argument can be summarized as follows: (1) The market assesses the expected return on capital goods. Once the banking system has settled the interest rate, the two aspects determine the price of investment goods. (2) Investment goods producers, given their production costs, decide the production volume, on the basis of those prices. (3) Given the estimates of expected returns, a rise in the interest rate will cut the price of capital goods, forcing producers to reduce the volume produced.

Thus the supply of new capital goods is regulated by the usual equation of costs and return, at the margin. Keynes did not distinguish between the net expected return on new capital goods and that on existing goods. On the proviso that there is no definite functional relationship between the net expected returns on new capital goods and the flow of new investment, their demand schedule is completely elastic to price. Thus a change in supply conditions, such as a rightward shift of the supply schedule resulting from a fall in costs, leads to more production which is completely absorbed at an unchanged price. This was the nature of the argument in the *Treatise* that changes in the price level for capital goods could come

---

4. Keynes, *Treatise*, in *C.W.K.* 5:180–81.

only from changes in the "tastes of the public" and in the "behaviour of the banking system."

Given the puzzles Keynes had already raised in earlier works, this theory of capital accumulation obviously was unsatisfactory. Although Kahn's criticism had not centered on the decision to invest, it did provoke Keynes to reexamine his doctrine at a vital point.

The realism of the logical schema of the *Treatise* was immediately subject to challenge by the Great Depression, an economic crisis of historical dimensions. To cope with unemployment the explanatory power of the fundamental equations was completely impotent, for they were based on the traditional assumption of constant real income with price level variations ensuing solely from an imbalance in the composition of output following basic changes in decisions to consume or to save. Any variations in total output and employment created by the imbalance would at most be temporary, and bound, sooner or later, to disappear. Investment, considered as the output of investment goods—that is, from the supply side—could only become imbalanced through the "feelings of the public" and the "behaviour of the banking system," elements that influenced the price of capital goods and the volume produced. As for the entrepreneurial spirit as the "motor of accumulation," its only part in the general framework of the *Treatise* was that latent in a vague propensity to increase (or to decrease) the level of economic activity in the presence of profits (or losses)—or imbalance between savings and investment.

What was it, however, that pushed the system to increase its stock of capital? What guarantees did entrepreneurs have that if they produced plant and machinery they could sell them at the same prices as the current existing stock of capital goods? What of the "fragility" of the capitalist accumulation mechanism if the demand for capital goods was relatively stable compared to consumption demand—that is, decisions to save?

In 1931, in the already pervasive atmosphere of world recession, Keynes gave a series of lectures in Chicago entitled *An Economic Analysis of Unemployment.*[5] Delivered with Keynes's usual descriptive effectiveness, the lectures nevertheless revealed the interpretative limitations of the *Treatise* schema. New elements began to emerge in Keynes's analysis, no longer confined within the

---

5. Reprinted in *C.W.K.*, vol. 13.

tight boundaries of the fundamental equations. Fresh prospects for future theoretical development beckoned.

Between 1925 and 1928, Keynes observed, Europe and the United States had witnessed extremely rapid investment. In the United States capital accumulation in the form of buildings and plant had been "prodigious" and "incredible," doubling that achieved between 1919 and 1922. The New York capital market had not only sustained this enormous accumulative effort financially, but had also underwritten international long-term loans, funded by short-term deposits of various capital-exporting countries. South American investment programs and industrial reconstruction in Germany had especially benefited from this financing. Accumulation had been rapid almost everywhere, from Australia to Russia, the only exception being Britain.

Apart from some sectoral bottlenecks, investment had been financed out of savings; inflationary pressures had been negligible. The benefits were highly visible: housing, electricity, roads, plant, transport. It was "extraordinary imbecility" to believe that all this constituted nothing more than a prelude to depression, and that the system could only be restored by a sufficiently long period of "liquidation" or universal bankruptcy:

> I do not take this view. I find the explanation of the current business losses, of the reduction of output, and of the unemployment which necessarily ensues on this not in the high level of investment which was proceeding up to the spring of 1929, but in the subsequent cessation of this investment. I see no hope of a recovery except in a revival of the high level of investment. And I do not understand how universal bankruptcy can do any good or bring us nearer to prosperity, except in so far as it may, by some lucky chance clear the boards for the recovery of investment.[6]

If the world recession ensued from a decline in investment, a remedy could only emerge from a recovery in capital formation. The *Treatise* theory of the "credit cycle" was a fairly good explanation: investment dropping to a level lower than savings induced losses which had discouraged productive activity, causing a further drop in investment, further losses, and so on. The issue was, however, to explain the initial fall in investment which was the starting

---

6. Ibid., p. 349.

link in the whole chain reaction. Keynes realized that to explain the crisis this was the crux.

Unfortunately, the schema of the *Treatise* was not particularly helpful. His assault, as now suggested, superceded the *Treatise* and opened the road toward an analysis in which the investment pivot was essentially *demand* for new capital goods. Among the various causes forestalling new accumulation Keynes cited the fact that "in the course of time all the best propositions had got taken up, and the cream was off the business."[7]

Investment opportunities depend on their expected return; once expectations become gloomy (relative to the rate of interest) investment falls. The probability of pessimism rises in concert with the volume of capital already in place. Keynes thereupon suggested that to insure recovery it was imperative to implement a policy of low long-term interest rates and to undertake public expenditure programs, and all for "the re-establishment of confidence." There was a more commonplace call for a relaxation in international tension through a moratorium on war debts; Keynes moreover asserted, however, that any expansive effects realized by other policies might well be "magnified" by a positive reaction on the "state of confidence."

The Chicago lecture revealed that Keynes had made another fundamental break with the theory of the *Treatise*. In examining the cumulative mechanism underlying the crisis, Keynes, while drawing on the fundamental equations, acknowledged that variations in real income and employment might be more than passing disequilibria pauses due to downward rigidity in money wages. In an explanation of the recession phase brought on by a fall in investment, unemployment is discerned in the light of its negative effects on purchasing power and consumption. The reduction of savings in the struggle to maintain living standards is seen as one channel through which savings and investment may be brought back into balance, halting the cumulative income debacle.[8]

To be sure, on this matter of variability of real income, there had been a cleavage between Keynes's theory and his policy prescriptions even prior to the publication of the *Treatise*. Evidence of the contradiction was contained in his pamphlet "Can Lloyd George Do It?" This was coauthored with Hubert Henderson to support

7. Ibid., p. 350.
8. Ibid., p. 356.

the Liberal party's program of public works, presented by Lloyd George during the 1929 General Elections campaign. The pamphlet had adopted a highly effective polemical tone. It had attacked the argument used by the government to oppose any serious program of public expenditure; on the other hand, it used arguments based more on good common sense than on established economic theory to explain why Lloyd George's "pledge" would actually work.

The government's position cited the inflationary dangers inherent in public expenditure and, more technically, the limited amount of employment that could be created for every one million pounds spent. On the first point, the pamphlet replied that it was absurd to dispense the "savings" of the community for paying unemployment benefits instead of having the jobless build houses, roads, and railroads, and thus raising income, wealth, and employment. The only possible circumstances in which public expenditure might incite inflation would be *if all available human and material resources were already fully employed.* With over one million unemployed, the threat of inflation was like "warning a patient who is wasting away from emaciation of the dangers of excessive corpulence."

As far as the volume of induced employment was concerned, there would be not only the jobs created *directly*, in the specific sectors of public expenditure, but also the jobs created *indirectly* in related sectors. Furthermore, any employment increase was bound to lead to cumulative activity as a result of expenditures by previously unemployed income-earners:

> The fact that many workpeople who are now unemployed would be receiving wages instead of unemployment pay would mean an increase in effective purchasing power which would give a general stimulus to trade. Moreover, the greater trade activity would make for further trade activity; for the forces of prosperity, like those of depression, work with a cumulative effect.[9]

These views are scarcely compatible with, and surely do not emanate from, the theory underlying the *Treatise*. Real incomes and employment (in the pamphlet) are disclosed as variables contingent on expenditure. In the argument on the cumulative effect of an initial income rise there is a glimmer of the *General Theory*: an initial verbal account of the investment multiplier.

---

9. "Can Lloyd George Do It?", p. 106.

The hypothesis of constant real income, used in the fundamental equations, had been vexing the young economists in the Cambridge "Circus": it became the critical target for them. Keynes, in his maturing perspective on the crisis, had already abandoned it, even prior to the official publication of the *Treatise*. Before he could shed the theoretical apparatus, however, he needed a more general analytical framework capturing the essense of the way the capitalist system actually worked, a step for which he was not yet prepared. Judging by his later development, and above all by the ground gained between the second half of 1931 and the final draft of the *General Theory*—a construction of a new theoretical framework piece by piece, proposition by proposition—the only defensible impression is that he was fully aware of the need to place the variability of income at the vital center of his analysis.

Yet he was conscious that this would shake the structure of the consolidated orthodox theory. Knocking out the concept of constant full-employment income meant an assault at the very roots of the theory from which "automatic" full employment derived its analytical sustenance. In particular, the fundamental problem Keynes had to solve—if he sought to make the variability of income the pivot of his analysis—was the refutation of the "classical" theory of interest.

Donald Moggridge has observed that there was a certain period in which the theoretical position of the young economists of the Cambridge "Circus" seemed more advanced than that of Keynes himself.[10] Reference here is not so much to the obvious complexities of a comparison of this kind, but rather to the fact that whenever the "Circus" managed to outrun Keynes, its success was limited to individual points rather than to their positioning in the full theory. One significant example concerned precisely the variations in income and employment created by bulges in public expenditure.

In June 1931 Kahn published his celebrated article whose aim was to "evaluate the repercussions in concrete terms" of an increase in domestic investment, or, more specifically, of expenditure on public works, on overall employment. Kahn separates the "primary" increase in employment, linked directly and indirectly to the new investment (e.g., road building), and the "secondary" increase in the consumer goods sector, caused by the expenditures of the new primary workers. The relationship between secondary and primary employment is a measure of the full benefit of the extra in-

---

10. Moggridge, ed., *C.W.K.* 13:342.

vestment flow. Supposing money wages stay unchanged, and that the central bank adopts a nonrestrictive stance—it does not intervene to block the expansion through credit restriction—Kahn calculates the number of "secondary" jobs created by each "primary" unit of employment.

Underlying this ingenious exercise is the hypothesis that the supply curve for consumer goods is perfectly elastic so that an increase in demand can be met by more output without a rise in costs and prices. The condition of the British economy, Kahn observed, was characterized by extraordinary unused capacity, adding realism to his assumption. With respect to the first fundamental equation of the *Treatise*, this implied that more investment need not necessarily force up the price level for consumer goods; income and savings could rise in such a way as to nullify any price effect of greater investment. Only after full employment would a price storm threaten and restore the force of the original interpretation of the equation.

Kahn's assessment of the employment "multiplier" and the analysis in "Can Lloyd George Do It?" are both attaching the same status to the impulse of more public expenditure on jobs. Kahn's contribution to Keynes's thinking represented an analytic quantum leap, for once an unequivocal relationship between employment and real income is established, the logical mechanism underlying the employment multiplier is unlocked in precisely the same fashion as in the *General Theory*'s income multiplier.

Keynes still had to find, in abandoning the assumption of constant income at full employment, the exact spot for inserting the multiplier into a general theory in which income could not only vary but could settle at diverse equilibrium levels. The multiplier itself, which measured the variation in employment (or income) caused by exogenous shifts in investment, could play only a limited part.

Thanks, at least in part, to the debate with Hayek, Keynes saw intuitively that crucial to sustaining the full employment assumption was the traditional theory of savings and investment equilibrium; this then had to be the salient from which to launch his assault. He detected this as the crucial point as early as the first drafts of what he referred to, in a letter to his mother (September 1932), as a "new book on monetary theory." Surviving still is a chapter entitled "The Parameters of a Monetary Economy," which Moggridge dates prior to the end of 1932.[11] Referring to other chapters and notes (of which we have no trace), Keynes draws a concise outline of a model which contains, in embryonic form, the fundamental propositions of what was to become the *General Theory*. The parameters include: the quantity of money, liquidity preference, expectations concerning the quasi-rent from capital goods, and the preference for present over future consumption (or consumption over savings).

The surviving chapter contains only a few lines on liquidity preference, which suggests it had already been discussed earlier. There is a clear outline of the idea of a functional relationship between the *demand* for liquid reserves and the interest rate, so that given the quantity of money (M), it is possible to calculate the rate of interest (ρ)

$$\rho = A(M)$$

in which A is the liquidity preference function.[12]

In his calculation of the price of capital goods (P_2) Keynes retained the same approach adopted in the *Treatise*. However, he opts more decisively than previously for the idea of expected net returns on capital goods (B), which, borrowing from Marshall's terminology, he calls "expected quasi-rents." Applying thereupon the analytical proposition for the equilibrium interest rate he is thus able to incorporate this as a discount rate, thereby freeing his theory from vague references to the "desires of the public" and to the "behaviour of the banking system."[13] Thus:

$$P_2 = B(\rho).$$

For a given supply curve for the sector (C), the production of capital goods (I') is determined by price P_2.

$$I' = C(P_2).$$

The public's time preference, the decision to consume (or to save), is applied in the determination of the prices of consumer goods. According to Keynes this implied a profound break with the

---

11. Ibid., pp. 397–405.

12. I have used the same symbols here as in Keynes's original.

13. The "desires of the public" are now expressed in the function A, and the "behaviour of the banking system" is lodged in the quantity of money M.

traditional theory of interest in which the interest rate is determined by savers' time preference, even if the precise mechanism is left vague. In his proposed theory, "what the general state of time preference directly determines at any moment is not the volume of investment but the *price level.*"[14]

Attaching values to the first three parameters, namely: (1) a given quantity of money, (2) a given liquidity preference, and (3) given expectations concerning quasi-rents, then the interest rate, the prices of investment goods,[15] and the volume of these goods produced are all determined.

At this stage in his thought, the public's time preference determined a volume of savings which, in equilibrium, must necessarily match the investment volume: the balance came via flux in the prices of consumer goods. At the bottom of this last proposition is the assumption that consumer goods output is *constant.* If so, once I' is settled, there follows the value of total output—and income. Any savings and investment discrepancy implies an imbalance between the demand and the (given) output of consumer goods and is entirely reflected in their price level. The adjustment operates through the effects on savings of the redistribution of income associated with profits and losses generated by the savings-investment gap. Thus, writing time preference as G, and consumer goods prices as P_1, Keynes writes:[16]

$$P_1 = G(I).$$

The four relations enable Keynes to determine the variables P_2, I' (and given the unit costs of production, I), and P_1 by recursion. Keynes specifies that his only aim in the equational formulation is to clarify the logic underlying the system: "These parameters themselves are not entirely independent of one another and the schedules expressing them should be stated in the form of simulta-

---

14. *C.W.K.* 13:401.

15. Keynes specifies that for both investment and consumption goods he has in mind a "complex of prices" rather than an average. The same applies for interest rates. He did not develop this analytical specification further.

16. Here, Keynes, rather than assuming capital goods to be valued at their cost of production (I'), takes them as being valued at sales price (I). His probable intention was to consider the influence on savings of profits in the capital goods sector. Taking P_2 as known, all that is necessary to pass from I' to I is to specify the unit cost of production.

neous equations," given that, "there is some measure of inter-dependence between all the elements of an economic system."[17]

As a first step he abandoned the hypothesis of a constant output of consumer goods, and the invariance of liquidity preference vis-à-vis different levels of prices and income. Thus the adjustment process between savings and income may operate not only via prices and income redistribution, but also through variations in output—an idea more fully embraced in the *General Theory*.

Reflecting on this first attempt by Keynes to move beyond the narrow confines of the *Treatise* and on to a more general theory of capitalism, emphasis must go to his rupture of the "neoclassical" theory of interest. This break should not be visualized in terms of the *Treatise's* analysis but rather against the traditional theory which already regarded the *Treatise* as genuinely heterodox. In the model just outlined, both the multiplier and variations in income play minor roles in equilibrating savings and investment: Keynes still seemed to hold, too often, the view that consumer goods output is constant. What can be discerned, however, is his concern with searching out a new theory of interest rate determination and his formulation of liquidity preference, which in embryo is incorporated in the *Treatise* in terms of (modern) "portfolio choice." The theory of interest appears thus as the core of his assault on traditional theory.

Reference will be made to this aspect later when we consider Keynes's critique of the "classical" theory of interest.[18] I should, however, immediately clarify the elements that lead me to suggest that the problem of interest rates was logically prior to income variations. The key question concerns the identification of the traditional theory of interest with respect to which Keynes intended to innovate in the model just described.

Consider the relationship between savings and investment contained in the fundamental equations. If $I(r)$ stands for the in-

---

17. *C.W.K.* 13:403, 405. This specification by Keynes shows that his vision of reality was by now incompatible with an interpretation of the *General Theory* strictly on the line of causal relationships. For an elaboration on a different line see L. Pasinetti, *Growth and Income Distribution: Essays in Economic Theory* (Cambridge: At the University Press, 1974).

18. When Keynes, in the *General Theory*, refers to the "classical economists," he is referring both to Ricardo and to the later "marginalist economists" (more commonly referred to today as the neoclassical school).

vestment function, $S(r,Y)$ for the savings function, r for the rate of interest, and Y for total income, equilibrium in the sense of the *Treatise*'s view of its constituent stable price level requires the condition $S(r,Y) = I(r)$.

Taking Y as determined by supply and demand equilibrium on the labor market, and at full employment, this balance is secured via variations in r. If Keynes had sought to depict a process of adjustment via income, within the framework of the *Treatise*, it would have been logical for him to argue that the interest rate was determined "elsewhere." Income, free of any tie with the notion of a real equilibrium wage, would move to balance off savings and investment. Both income variability and the multiplier could have taken center stage, with the rate of interest determined "elsewhere," by some other theory, and being simply a means to an end.

In the Hayek controversy, however, Keynes reproached the new Austrian monetary economists with their conception of traditional theory. On this conception, if the quantity of money was constant, investment was always *identical* to savings. What he intended to criticize was thus that:

$$S(r,Y) = I.$$

The significance of this is that the level of investment becomes a *variable* (I).

Because in this formulation savings and investment are equal for any value of Y, it is not enough to single out *one* equilibrium level of income, even if it is conceded that the interest rate is determined "elsewhere." The only escape route from *indeterminacy* would be to take refuge in the notion of *constant* full employment income.

In his denying the realism of this hypothesis—the shaft for which the *General Theory* is notorious—Keynes's innovative task required that he prove its logical flaw. Once the decision was made to abandon the stipulation of full employment equilibrium, Keynes saw starkly that the fundamental question was not the rate of interest as descending from some other theory, but that of demonstrating that the prevailing traditional theory was logically untenable.

CHAPTER 8

THE GENERAL THEORY: CONSUMPTION, INVESTMENT, AND EFFECTIVE DEMAND

Leaping forward from the schema traced in the chapter on the parameters of a monetary economy, Keynes made the traditional theory of full employment his target; this is confirmed by the various drafts of the index for the new book, which he now referred to as *The General Theory of Employment*.

The first complete index is dated December 1933; a second draft, which precedes the preparation of the first proofs and which closely follows the final plan of the work, dates to mid 1934.[1] Like the final edition, both contain a first book which is preoccupied with the postulates of classical theory and which then compares these with the essential features of the new theoretical message of the *General Theory*. It was very clearly Keynes's intention to immediately confront the reader with the flawed foundation of the traditional theory; later on he would illustrate the points, showing the substance of his rejection in a complete interpretative schema of the functioning of a capitalist economy.

The classical theory of value and production, as Keynes remarks at the very beginning of *The General Theory of Employment, Interest and Money*,[2] has been primarily concerned with the determination of the exchange relationships among the goods produced and the allocation of factors of production, for a given volume of employed resources. Its vulnerability lies in its failure to examine the forces which *determine* employment, perhaps because "the fun-

---

1. Cf. *C.W.K.* 13:421–23.
2. (London: Macmillan, 1936); reprinted in *C.W.K.*, vol. 7.

damental theory underlying it has been deemed so simple and obvious that it has received, at the most, a bare mention."[3] The theory relies on two fundamental postulates never seriously questioned: (1) Wages are equal to the marginal product of labor, and (2) the utility of wages, for a given quantity of labor employed, is equal to the marginal disutility of that same amount of employment.[4]

The first postulate, derived from the hypothesis that entrepreneurs maximize their profits, enables the classical theory to derive its demand function for labor, namely, its marginal product curve. Following the law of diminishing returns (under constant quantities of other factors) marginal products fall as employment rises.

The second postulate serves to isolate a supply function for labor which posits more effort as real wages rise: the utility of real wages must, in equilibrium, counterbalance the growing disutility of extra work. The second postulate went back at least as far as W. Stanley Jevons, who drew the appropriate functions.

The level of employment corresponding to this equilibrium is stipulated as "full employment," which the classical theory held to be compatible with both frictional unemployment due to systemic delays in the adjustment process and various imperfections in the labor market, and "voluntary unemployment," stemming from claims for real wages in excess of productivity.

According to classical theory, employment increases must wait upon the shifting of the labor demand function, or the supply function, or both, either through an increase in productivity or from a decreased disutility or lessened work-aversion of labor. In the early 1930s, Keynes observed, it was difficult to deny that a greater volume of labor was available for jobs *at current real wages* if a higher labor demand prevailed.

How could this be reconciled with the second postulate? The classical theory's reply was that labor-hire was limited because real wages were too high. If workers accepted a reduction in money wages this would in turn cut real wages and induce greater labor-hire. By slashing money wages sufficiently real wages would become compatible, at the margin, with the marginal disutility of labor, both postulates would be satisfied, and full employment would rule.

---

3. *General Theory*, in C.W.K. 7:4–5.
4. Ibid., p. 5.

Keynes's expression of disagreement built two arches, the first covering the way workers "actually behaved" in wage bargaining, and the second, the "theoretically fundamental" one, the forces that determine real wages.

On the first point, Keynes invokes historical experience of the recent and more distant past, declaring that while workers resist reductions in money wages they are *not* unwilling to work for lower real wages in the form of higher consumer goods prices: "In other words, it may be the case that within a certain range the demand of labour is for a minimum money-wage and not for a minimum real wage."[5]

This, however, argues from an empirical position describing workers' behavior. Although it would be odd to argue that under the massive unemployment of the Great Depression an increase in the cost-of-living would induce labor supply withdrawal, there are other contingencies that might violate any fast rule.

This was not the essential objection. The classical adjustment mechanism was based on a conviction that workers could implement a specific real wage consequent of their bargaining with employers. It was roundly agreed that bargaining is actually conducted over money wages; nonetheless, the classicist was convinced that each level of money wages implies a different corresponding real wage; the idea was that real and money wages moved in tandem.

Keynes thought this was rather strange reasoning, for in classical theory price depended on marginal production costs, measured in money, which were composed mainly of wages. It follows that wages and prices should decline together so that a money wage cut would leave real wages unaltered! To Keynes the proposition that labor was able to control real wages had been espoused "by its being confused with the proposition that labour is always in a position to determine what real wages shall correspond to *full* employment, i.e. the *maximum* quantity of employment which is compatible with a given real wage."[6] Keynes's thesis was: "There may exist no expedient by which labour as a whole can reduce its *real* wage to a given figure by making revised *money* bargains with entrepreneurs." Keynes's argument has become one of the most original contributions of the *General Theory* to economic thought as com-

---

5. Ibid., p. 8.
6. Ibid., p. 12.

pared to the prevailing, and still commonplace, neoclassical confusions.

This point is directly tied to the question, raised at the end of the previous chapter, about the logical priority that Keynes accorded to his critique of the traditional theory of savings and investment equilibrium. Keynes felt that he had to lay bare the hollow underlying structure of the classical edifice. He realized that the second postulate would only topple if he succeeded in undermining the series of propositions that gave it cohesiveness. He did not doubt that the idea of a continuous adjustment of demand to production rested on Say's Law, according to which "supply creates its own demand":

> From the time of Say and Ricardo the classical economists have taught that supply creates its own demand;—meaning by this in some significant, but not clearly defined, sense that the whole of the costs of production must necessarily be spent in the aggregate, directly or indirectly, on purchasing the product.[7]

Among later economists this law was inculcated by John Stuart Mill and by Marshall in his first writings. In Marshall's later works, as in Edgeworth and Pigou: "The doctrine is never stated in this crude form. Nevertheless it still underlies the whole classical theory, which would collapse without it."[8] Contemporary economists thus end up in incoherence. On the one hand, the economic situation clearly proves the proposition's unrealism, leading to conclusions contradicting their theories; on the other, however, they rebel at discarding the theory. One reason for the retention lies in the apparent good sense lurking behind the idea that costs are always covered by sales revenues, and thus that savings automatically translated into investment must necessarily enrich the community. It was not to be precluded, however, that the apparent common sense also carried a confusion with another identity, namely, between total income and the value of production made equal by the accounting definition of the two aggregates. In any case, for classical theory "all the rest follows—the social advantage of private and national thrift, the traditional attitude towards the rate of interest,

---

7. Ibid., p. 18.
8. Ibid., p. 19.

the classical theory of unemployment, the quantity theory of money, the unqualified advantages of *laissez-faire* in respect of foreign trade and much else we shall have to question."[9]

Keynes quickly runs past most readers by injecting, with no preparation, the concepts of "aggregate demand and aggregate supply."[10] First, he discards his definition of profit used in the *Treatise*, considering it in the more congenial accounting fashion as the residual separating entrepreneurs' costs and returns, and as a component in total income.[11] Aggregate demand is defined as the proceeds that entrepreneurs *expect* from a given level of employment. In other words, the decision to employ a certain number of workers generates income while expenditure generates demand through decisions by households to consume and decisions by enterprises to invest. There is no automatic mechanism to guarantee that these demand decisions will aggregate to a sum equal to full employment income and production value. Rather the contrary: for consumption the tendency is to advance by a lesser proportion than income. Thus as employment goes up aggregate demand can only be aligned with full employment income if investment fills the growing gap between consumption and full employment income. Aggregate supply (or, "the aggregate supply price of the output of a given amount of employment") is defined as "the expectation of proceeds which will just make it worth the while of the entrepreneurs to give that employment," that is, to cover production costs and insure a margin of profit.

Both demand and aggregate supply are thus functions of employment. The aggregate demand function, written as $D = f(N)$, where D is demand and N the number employed, ascends at a diminishing rate owing to consumer behavior. Under conditions of diminishing marginal productivity, the aggregate supply function,

9. Ibid., p. 21.

10. On these concepts see S. Weintraub, *An Approach to the Theory of Income Distribution* (Philadelphia and New York: Chilton Books, 1958), for an early and fairly complete statement of what Keynes appeared to intend.

11. Among the costs of production Keynes includes not only the expenditures necessary for the services of productive factors but also the intra-firm purchases and the "user-cost" of plant and equipment. Subsequently, to simplify the analysis, however, these two items of cost are suppressed from both aggregate costs and aggregate receipts.

$Z = \Phi(N)$ (where Z = supply), accelerates as N increases. Equilibrium employment will be established at a level of N where $D = Z$ or where $f(N) = \Phi(N)$. The value of aggregate demand at the intersection $D = Z$ is called by Keynes "effective demand."[12]

Given the expenditure behavior of households and firms, that is, hypothesizing a specific aggregate demand curve, effective demand is centered at a unique point on the aggregate supply curve. Conversely, according to Say's Law in classical theory, namely, that "supply always creates its own demand," both D and Z merge, forming not separate tracks but a single track.[13] Keynes's equilibrium can come at *any* level of employment, and full employment is only a fortuitous outcome: it would be contingent on the second postulate's being satisfied. Normally, then, real wages will exceed the marginal disutility of labor.

Keynes digresses and pauses to reflect on the fundamental importance of the effective demand concept. This derived from Malthus who vainly sought, in correspondence with Ricardo, to persuade the latter of the danger to production of a demand shortfall. Malthus failed, Ricardo succeeded, and the concept of aggregate demand was silenced:

> Ricardo conquered England as completely as the Holy Inquisition conquered Spain. Not only was his theory accepted by the city, by statesmen and by the academic world. But controversy ceased; the other point of view completely disappeared; it ceased to be discussed. The great puzzle of effective demand with which Malthus had wrestled vanished from economic literature. You will not find it mentioned even once in the whole works of Marshall, Edgeworth and Professor Pigou, from whose hands the classical theory has re-

---

12. The relation between the Z-function and profit-maximizing precepts is tricky and worked out with obscurity by Keynes, except on the most sympathetic reading. Cf. S. Weintraub, "The Micro-Foundations of Aggregate Demand and Supply," *The Economic Journal*, September 1957. D. Patinkin assigns most credit for this interpretation of Keynes to Weintraub, declaring Keynes was more in error than obscure (*Anticipations of the General Theory* [Oxford: Blackwell, 1982]).

13. Although effective demand corresponds to the one point on the aggregate demand curve which intersects a distinct supply curve, in the following pages the terms *aggregate* and *effective demand* will be used in the same way as Keynes often used them, as synonyms indicating the complex of decisions to spend, depending on income and other variables.

ceived its most mature embodiment. It could only live on furtively, below the surface, in the underworlds of Karl Marx, Silvio Gesell or Major Douglas.[14]

Keynes hardly did more than take passing notice of the aggregate supply function; somehow it was dimly related to Marshall's industry supply curves with their underlying cost curve aspect. His focus was on the aggregate demand function as the cornerstone of his new theoretical model. It was incumbent then for him to find rigorous and realistic confirmation for his long-time insistence that decisions to invest and decisions to consume are independent and that in some independent conjunction they determine the effective level of employment.

As a component of aggregate demand, consumption should be capable of being expressed as a function of (N). Positing an approximately stable relationship between employment and income,[15] Keynes took consumption, expressed in wage units (C_w), as a function of income, also in wage units (Y_w). Thus $C_w = f(Y_w)$; alternatively, where W stands for the wage unit,[16] $C = Wf(Y_w)$.

This is, by now, the famous and widely used "propensity to consume." It formally encapsulates the complex of objective and subjective motives which guide individuals in making decisions on using income to satisfy immediate or future consumption needs.

Keynes listed a series of subjective motives, including the desire to protect against unforeseen needs or to enjoy a gradually higher

---

14. Keynes, *General Theory*, in *C.W.K.* 7:32.

15. As the elasticity of production to employment varies from sector to sector, changes in the sectoral composition of output can affect the relation between jobs and income. Keynes postponed discussion of it until his chapter 20, and there it is discussed only briefly and is vaguely tied to his macrotheory. Cf. Weintraub, *Approach to the Theory of Income Distribution*, chap. 2.

16. By the "wage-unit" Keynes means the money-wage of the "labor-unit": "taking an hour's employment of ordinary labour as our unit and weighting an hour's employment of special labor in proportion to its remuneration" (*General Theory*, in *C.W.K.* 7:41). Keynes works in money magnitudes deflated by the wage-unit and thus seeks relief from ambiguities of quantitative notions as real income and price level: "In dealing with the theory of employment I propose, therefore, to make use of only two fundamental units of quantity, namely, quantities of money-value and quantities of employment" (ibid., p. 41).

living standard or to acquire a sense of independence or to leave a legacy—or some pure blend of greed. Motives evolve out of the social and institutional organization, including moral and religious convictions, and tend to change almost imperceptibly over time. Withal, the subjective factors underlying "the propensity to consume" are regarded as stable. Modifications in the distribution of wealth, which could alter consumption, could be precluded insofar as substantial movements *might* occur within society only over very long periods of time.

The propensity to consume is also subject to a series of "objective factors" which may entail a different consumption intake at the same income level. In formal terms this would involve either a shift in the simple functional relationship specified, or the inclusion of new independent variables besides income. Keynes lists the following contingencies:

(a) *A change in the wage-unit.* It is not unreasonable to suppose that variations in consumers' income, expressed in wage-units, can vary consumption expenditure. Expressing income by E, so that $E = WN$, then money consumption outlay is a function that can be expressed as $C = f(E) = f(WN)$. Consumption, in wage-units C_w, may similarly be written: $C_w = f(N)$.

(b) *A change in the difference between gross income and net income.* For Keynes, for production decisions, gross income is the appropriate concept. Decisions to consume, however, depend on some concept of net income available to consumers, for example, total income net of depreciation.[17] Thus the income variable included in the consumption function must be net income. If the gap between gross and net income holds tight then either income category can be applied. But the discrepancy is bound to vary with employment fluctuations.

(c) *Windfall changes in wealth, not included in the calculation of net income.* Precisely because they are unforeseen and completely independent of income, changes in the value of real assets may be an important factor changing the propensity to consume.

(d) *Changes in the rate of time-discounting.* These are reflected not only in the interest rate but also in the expected rate of inflation and in risks for the future. In practice, however, Keynes

17. A detailed analysis of disposable income would also have to take account of firms' net savings and of direct taxation.

limited himself to considering variations in the interest rate, the direct effect of which on consumption he held to be negligible, resulting as they did from "countervailing tendencies." This was clearly the opposite of the view of traditional theory. He did believe that there could be a significant indirect effect via changes in the prices of shares, bonds, and other assets, and thus in the current value of wealth. These, however, could be included among the factors already listed in point (c).

(e) *Changes in fiscal policy.* The significance of these for consumption comes out of their impact on net income and on any draining of capital gains. Fiscal policies aimed at redistributing income can also influence the consumption-income relation.

(f) *Changes in the expected relation between present and future income.* These changes are relevant to the relation between expected flows of income and consumption needs over time.[18] Keynes believes that at the aggregate level the influence of these changes on individual consumption might balance out and be of negligible importance.

Overall, consumption is deemed to be a relatively stable function of income, with exceptions for unforeseen variations in wealth, significant interest rate lurches, or changes in fiscal policy. Keynes asserted: "The fundamental psychological law . . . is that men are disposed, as a rule and on the average, to increase their consumption as their income increases, but not by as much as the increase in their income."[19] In other words,

$$1 > \frac{dC_w}{dY_w} > 0.$$

The hypothesis is confirmed in cycles whether income increases or decreases. One could surmise that as income increases a growing proportion of income is saved, that is, that there is a declining marginal propensity to consume. This hypothesis is less cer-

---

18. Developments on this line of analysis—the "life cycle" hypothesis of A. Ando and F. Modigliani ("The Life Cycle Hypothesis of Savings: Aggregate Implications and Tests," *American-Economic Review*, March 1963); and the "permanent income" hypothesis of M. Friedman—were foreshadowed in Keynes.

19. *General Theory*, in C.W.K. 7:96.

tain and less essential for the qualitative analysis of the effects of decisions to spend on employment directions.

Positing a stable consumption function, the *General Theory* invokes investment fluctuations as inducing variations in income. Utilizing the concept of the marginal propensity to consume, Keynes was now able to give quantitative expression to his 1929 assessment of the direct and indirect effects of an autonomous increase in investment expenditure. For the analytical formulation he was able to draw on Kahn's equation for the "employment multiplier," now transformed into an investment multiplier.

Writing investment in wage units as I_w, Keynes partitions an increase in output between consumption and investment: $\Delta Y_w = \Delta C_w + \Delta I_w$. Remembering that in Keynes's terminology the marginal propensity to consume ($\Delta C_w / \Delta Y_w$) is written as $1 - 1/k$, one thus obtains

$$\Delta Y_w = (1 - 1/k)\,\Delta Y_w + \Delta I_w,$$

from which it follows that

$$\Delta Y_w = k\Delta I_w.$$

ΔY_w is an index of variation in real income, which is invariably k times the variation in investment: "k" is the "investment multiplier."[20]

As Keynesian textbooks came to teach, the higher the marginal propensity to consume the larger the multiplier effect: the multiplier tends to infinity as ($\Delta C_w / \Delta Y_w$) approximates unity: a stable, nonexplosive process requires

$$\frac{dC_w}{dY_w} < 1.$$

A decline in the marginal ratio as Y_w grows will compress the multiplier.

---

20. The investment multiplier will equal the employment multiplier if there is a stable relation between total output and total employment. This entails that the same relation must hold between these variables in each sector of the economy, thus insuring that the aggregate relation is independent of variations in the composition of output. Keynes declares there is "no reason to expect any material relevant difference in the shapes of the aggregate supply function for industry as a whole and for the investment industries respectively" (ibid., p. 116 n. 1).

Apart from the precise formula, the significance of the relationship between ΔY and ΔI lies in the fact that a bulge in I enhances income and output, thereby creating an equivalent amount of savings—*always*. It is in this sense that Keynes considers savings as being *determined* by investment; this allows him to strike the *coup de grâce* against traditional theory: insofar as higher interest rates cut investment, savings fall rather than rise.

The relationship obviously depends on the hypothesis that there exists a margin of plant and labor sufficient to sate the aggregate demand increases without obstructive bottlenecks.[21] In terms of the traditional theory of employment, the complete operation of the multiplier presumes a situation of underemployment—as was surely true in the Great Depression. To insure more output rather than a rise in prices, consumer goods producers would have to anticipate the new demand induced from the higher investment activity. Where the increase in employment in the investment sector is completely unexpected

> the efforts of those newly employed in the capital-goods industries to consume a proportion of their increased incomes will raise the prices of consumption-goods until a temporary equilibrium between demand and supply has been brought about partly by the high prices causing a postponement of consumption, partly by a redistribution of income in favour of the saving classes as an effect of the increased profits resulting from the higher prices, and partly by the higher prices causing a depletion of stocks.[22]

Referring back to Kahn's analysis, Keynes notes that the size of the multiplication process will depend on: (1) how the expenditure is financed, for example, whether the monetary policy will be more expansive, or otherwise interest rates may mount and cut into other investment; (2) private business confidence or fears engendered by state intervention or spending which may increase liquidity preference or deter investment; and (3) the economy's "openness,"

---

21. J. R. Hicks makes much of this point in stressing the availability of inventories of imported materials. See Hicks, *Crisis in Keynesian Economics* (Oxford: Blackwell, 1974).

22. Ibid., pp. 123–24. This passage indicates that Keynes did not neglect the problem detected by Hicks in *Crisis*.

the propensity to import: imports can mean a smaller domestic stimulus by "leaks" which benefit foreign industry.

In the Great Depression environment the implications of the multiplier analysis gave creditable theoretical underpinning to an economic policy promoting an expansion of public expenditure. As far as the outlets for public investment were concerned, Keynes did not have to repeat himself: he had already stated on many occasions that it was possible to build houses, roads, port infrastructures, and telephone networks, and to intervene in those intangible and unprofitable sectors which could benefit private enterprise and were crucial for long-run economic development, for example, education, research, and projects that yielded distant and uncertain returns. Educated as it was in classical economics, the political elite was unable to visualize these investments as providing an opportunity not only to reduce unemployment but also to enhance the wealth of the nation. Then came Keynes's bitterly ironical conclusion:

> Pyramid-building, earthquakes, even wars may serve to increase wealth, if the education of our statesmen on the principles of the classical economics stands in the way of anything better.
>
> It is curious how common sense, wriggling for an escape from absurd conclusions, has been apt to reach a preference for *wholly* "wasteful" forms of loan expenditure rather than for *partly* wasteful forms, which, because they are not wholly wasteful, tend to be judged on strict "business" principles. For example, unemployment relief financed by loans is more readily accepted than the financing of improvements at a charge below the current rate of interest; whilst the form of digging holes in the ground known as gold-mining, which not only adds nothing whatever to the real wealth of the world but involves the disutility of labour, is the most acceptable of all solutions.[23]

Decisions to invest are autonomous or wholly independent of decisions to consume and thus to save. Keynes does not have to elaborate further the fundamental nature of investment decisions for the capitalist system; it is these decisions that determine the accumulation of capital. There had already been the elaboration in the *Treatise* and in Keynes's controversy with Hayek. The *General Theory* concentrates on a more rigorous behavioral and formal anal-

23. *General Theory*, in *C.W.K.* 7:129.

ysis of the mechanism underlying decisions to accumulate. It should be recalled that in the *Treatise* the price of capital goods was determined exclusively by the public's financial options and by the behavior of the banks in supplying deposits, and thus the volume of investment depended on the supply curve for the sector. This invoked supply rather than demand, leaving vague the way in which entrepreneurial decisions to purchase new machinery and plant entered the accumulation process. Do these decisions shape the portfolio equilibrium responsible for the prices of new and old capital goods? Need they not be distinguished from savers' financial options? The answers were obscure, for the *Treatise* mainly evaded the problem despite Keynes's discernment of profit as the motor of accumulation.

The debate with Hayek, the prodding by Kahn and Robinson, and his own reflections on the Great Depression compelled Keynes to attend more deeply to the ultimate objective and subjective conditions, and the structural foundations relevant to the decisions to invest in a capitalist society. The novel and wholly original idea, around which the whole *General Theory* revolves, is that capital accumulates only insofar as entrepreneurs brave the pervasive uncertainty about the future and *act* to erect new productive facilities or to improve old ones putting aside doubts and skepticism or pessimistic clouds. The object of the entrepreneurs' evaluation is the series of annuities $(Q_1, Q_2, \ldots Q_n)$—the "prospective yield"—which they expect to obtain from a given investment project. A final comparison must then be made with the market "supply price" for the capital goods which will have to be purchased by the project, by "supply price" meaning "not the market price at which an asset of the type in question can actually be purchased in the market, but the price which would just induce a manufacturer newly to produce an additional unit of such assets."

The comparison between the prospective yield and the supply price reveals the rate of return, or what Keynes calls the "marginal efficiency of capital," which is the rate of discount "which would make the present value of the series of annuities given by the returns expected from the capital-asset during its life just equal to its supply price."[24]

Keynes insists that the operative terms in this comparison are

---

24. Ibid., p. 135.

the *current* cost of production of new capital goods and *expected* yield, rather than the historical cost and the current yield of an existing asset. The marginal efficiency of capital should not be confused with the current rate of profit, and surely not with past profit rates. Likewise, the marginal efficiency has to be distinguished from the marginal cost of using the machinery, or Keynes's notion of marginal "user cost." The relation between the marginal efficiency of capital and various hypothetical levels of investment—which is the crucial element in determining the investment activity actually undertaken by entrepreneurs—thus rests on the supply price of capital goods and expected yield, with each a function of the investment volume.[25]

Keynes falls back on the traditional hypothesis of a rising supply price ("diminishing returns") as the investment volume advances. On the relation of expected yield to investment he limits himself to the statement that "the prospective yield will fall as the supply of that type of capital is increased."

Keynes concludes that "the actual rate of current investment will be pushed to the point where there is no longer any class of capital-asset of which the marginal efficiency exceeds the current rate of interest."[26] A fall in the rate of interest leads, therefore, to an increase in the volume of investment, completely in line with traditional theory. In contrast to the neoclassical paradigm, Keynes is adamant in declaring that the marginal efficiency of capital should not be understood as a relationship between *physical* quantities of capital and product. Reference to the marginal physical productivity of capital "involves difficulties as to the definition of the physical unit of capital, which I believe to be both insoluble and unnecessary . . . [and] I know no means of reducing this to an intelligible arithmetical relation which does not bring in values."[27] Keynes's marginal efficiency is thus a value relation but it is free of the errors committed by the neoclassical economists and unearthed by recent criticism.[28] The neoclassical theory had too often linked a falling

25. For a systematic diagrammatic treatment of the tricky analysis see S. Weintraub, "The Marginal Efficiency of Capital and Its Supply Price," *Journal of Post-Keynesian Economics*, Winter 1983.

26. *General Theory*, in *C.W.K.* 7:136.

27. Ibid., p. 138.

28. For this point see P. Garegnani, "Heterogeneous Capital, the Production Function and the Theory of Distribution," *The Review of Economic Studies*, July 1970.

marginal productivity to a *value* quantity of heterogeneous capital. Keynes never fell into this trap. His flow of net returns is a subjective projection into the future, grounded in expectations concerning not only quantity of product but also sales and costs, especially the evolution of wages which are the chief component of variable costs directly and in materials purchased.[29] This amounts to saying that marginal efficiency is related to investment projects where capital is not the only factor subject to change, so that marginal productivity is anyway meaningless.

As an uncommon twist, at the time, Keynes's notion of marginal efficiency also caught *prospective* price changes. Expectation of a rise in price levels would elevate marginal efficiency: if interest rates were constant, the demand for investment might thus be swayed.

It is this link between inflationary (or deflationary) expectations and marginal efficiency that Keynes argues as underlying the analysis, proffered by Irving Fisher,[30] of the nominal and the real rate of interest where the latter is defined as the algebraic sum of the nominal rate and the expected rate of variation in prices. According to Keynes's explanation, the Fisher analysis stopped just short of stressing how variations in future prices affected current activity, and the distinction between whether they are foreseen or not. If anticipated fully, variations in future prices will have no effect whatsoever: they will only induce the public to shift from money (and financial) to real assets, raising thereby the *nominal* rate of interest and the current price of real assets with a consequent cut in their return, so that "the advantages of holding money and holding goods are again equalised."

If inflationary expectations are to affect current decisions to invest in new capital goods rather than exhausting their perturbations in a process of portfolio adjustment whereby a new equilibrium is achieved between the nominal rate, as corrected for inflation, and the rate on real assets, they will have to exert a direct influence over the incentive to invest through the marginal efficiency of cap-

---

29. In his discussion of the "nature of capital" in chapter 16, Keynes observes: "If capital becomes less scarce, the excess yield will diminish, without its having become less productive—at least in the physical sense" (p. 213).

30. *The Theory of Interest* (1930; reprint, New York: Kelley and Millan, 1954).

ital. Since expected variations in the value of money are bound to affect the price of existing capital goods, the Fisher effect is not ignored. As the increase in the marginal efficiency of capital will also stimulate demand for, and thus the production of, new capital goods, the expansionary momentum will dominate so long as the increase in the nominal rate of interest is less than that in the marginal efficiency of capital.

The crucial nature of expectations in determining investment demand is apparent.[31] Its *modus operandi* comes through the marginal efficiency of capital which denotes the net rate of return which entrepreneurs conjecture will evolve during the life of their new capital goods. Keynes concurs that these expectations are partly based on past events, that is, on facts known at least with some certainty, and on future events which only lend themselves to forecasts, projected with far less confidence. The facts we do know include the existing stock of "various types of capital-assets . . . and the strength of the existing consumers' demand for goods which require for their efficient production a relatively larger assistance from capital."[32] Future unforeseen matters include quantitative and qualitative changes in capital goods, consumer tastes, the intensity of effective demand, and the flux in money wages. Most important here is the "state of long-term expectations," as opposed to the short-term "daily" expectations which, according to Keynes, influence production decisions under existing productive capacity.

How are our long-term expectations molded? Is there a rational or logical basis? In Keynes's exposition of marginal efficiency these questions arise spontaneously. Yet to appreciate the stance of the *General Theory* it is well to recall that he had pondered the issues in the *Treatise on Probability* and in discourse with eminent logicians such as Ludwig Wittgenstein and Frank Ramsey, who were friends and colleagues at Cambridge.[33]

---

31. Cf. the fine survey and restatement by G. L. S. Shackle, "New Tracks for Economic Theory, 1926–1939," in *Modern Economic Thought*, ed. S. Weintraub (Philadelphia: University of Pennsylvania Press, 1977).

32. *General Theory*, in *C.W.K.* 7:147.

33. The Austrian philosopher Wittgenstein has been universally recognized for his contribution to logic and the foundations of mathematics. He had been attracted to Cambridge by his fascination with the work conducted there by Bertrand Russell. Keynes assisted in getting him a

Expectations immediately conjure images of a *probabilistic* analysis of risk and uncertainty. In his *Treatise on Probability* Keynes had distinguished between "risky" events, whose probability distribution is known, and "uncertain" events, whose probability distribution is unknown. In the *General Theory* he invokes this distinction, arguing that since it would be unthinkable to submit economic activity to a planned series of experiments from which to derive frequency distributions, then the economic facts that are the object of forecasting are in nature uncertain. Ramsey, however, had criticized certain sections of the *Treatise*, making a distinction between "human" and "formal" logic. The latter has, as its object, the rules of coherent reasoning, while human logic consists of certain "useful mental habits" whereby the mind sifts the information provided via perception, memory, and other channels to achieve some knowledge of truth.

In a review article, published a few years after Ramsey's premature death, Keynes acknowledged the fecundity of this distinction in erecting a probability calculus:

> The application of these ideas to the logic of probability is very fruitful. Ramsey argues, as against the view which I had put forward, that probability is concerned not with objective relations between propositions but (in some sense) with degrees of belief, and he succeeds in showing that the calculus of probabilities simply amounts to a set of rules for ensuring that the system of degrees of belief which we hold shall be a *consistent* system. Thus the calculus of probabilities belongs to formal logic. But the basis of our degrees of

---

teaching post. Wittgenstein expressed his gratitude to Frank Ramsey for "innumerable conversations during the last two years of his life" and to Piero Sraffa for the criticism "which for many years he constantly focussed on my thought" (Wittgenstein, preface to *Philosophical Investigation* [Oxford: Basil Blackwell, 1953]).

Ramsey, a fellow at King's College who died at the age of twenty-six, was described by Keynes as a genius whose gifts "have been taken from us at the height of their excellence and before their harvest of work and life could be gathered in." His incursions into economic theory included his "optimal savings" theory which was judged by Keynes as "one of the most remarkable contributions to mathematical economics ever made." See Keynes, "F. P. Ramsey as an Economist," *The Economic Journal* (1930); reprinted in *C.W.K.* 10:335–36; and Ramsey, "A Mathematical Theory of Saving," *The Economic Journal*, December 1928.

belief—or the *a priori* probabilities, as they used to be called—is part of our human outfit, perhaps given us merely by natural selection, analogous to our perceptions and our memories rather than to formal logic. So far I yield to Ramsey—I think he is right.[34]

There is an echo of this confession when Keynes states that the state of long-term expectations depends not only on what is viewed as being most probable, but also on the "confidence" attached to these views: more intellectual courage is needed in confronting uncertain events than in dealing with merely risky ones. "Human logic" can thus override "formal logic" in comprehending the intricate and subtle mechanisms underlying the "state of confidence," a complex of conditions to which businessmen attach great importance in their decision-making and which economists, despite its influence at the vital nerve-center of the marginal efficiency of capital and thus on investment, have never dissected with either rigor or rapt attention.

Keynes, however, reluctantly admits that "there is, however, not much to be said about the state of confidence *a priori*" and that "our conclusions must mainly depend upon the actual observations of markets and business psychology."[35] Nonetheless, it is a fact that for many investments whose useful lifespan is long there are very few objective elements on which to base an earnings forecast. As a consequence, especially in the past when capital ownership and actual control were fused, investment partook of the nature of "a lottery." As the outcome of the game could not be subject to the law of large numbers, the play depended on the "confidence" of the entrepreneurial spirit: "If human nature felt no temptation to take a chance, no satisfaction (profit apart) in constructing a factory, a railway, a mine or a farm, there might not be much investment merely as a result of cold calculations."[36]

The then apparent separation between ownership and control, and the parallel development of stock markets, have significantly altered the game, improving it in some respects and deadening it in others. The possibility of selling shares on the Stock Exchange can increase their liquidity, with an undoubtedly positive effect on the propensity to invest. The Stock Exchange, moreover, is omni-

34. *C.W.K.* 13:338–39.
35. *General Theory*, in *C.W.K.* 7:149.
36. Ibid., p. 150.

present in the calculations of entrepreneurs or those contemplating real investment:

> But the daily revaluations of the Stock Exchange, though they are primarily made to facilitate transfers of old investments between one individual and another, inevitably exert a decisive influence on the rate of current investment. For there is no sense in building up a new enterprise at a cost greater than that at which a similar existing enterprise can be purchased; whilst there is an inducement to spend on a new project what may seem an extravagant sum, if it can be floated off on the Stock Exchange at an immediate profit.[37]

Keynes is reiterating here that a high price quotation on the Stock Exchange "involves an increase in the marginal efficiency of the corresponding type of capital" and thus will facilitate investment. It follows that Stock Exchange quotations are an element modifying expectations concerning the net *expected* income from investment projects in new capital goods of the same kind. It also ensues, however, that as the Stock Exchange often assesses the situation through the eyes of the short-sighted speculator rather than the long-range investor, this influence may have a negative outcome.

The Stock Exchange, or more precisely the expectations of Stock Exchange operators, as an element in the state of confidence injects a reference point for molding expectations on the net return from new investment. These, however, rest strongly on a "convention" that "the existing state of affairs will continue indefinitely, except in so far as we have specific reasons to expect a change," and the convention is an extremely "precarious" one, also owing to speculation:

> It might have been supposed that competition between expert professionals, possessing judgment and knowledge beyond that of the average private investor, would correct the vagaries of the ignorant individual left to himself. It happens, however, that the energies and skill of the professional investor and speculator are mainly occupied otherwise. For most of these persons are, in fact, largely concerned, not with making superior long-term forecasts of the probable yield of an investment over its whole life, but with foresee-

---

37. Ibid., p. 151.

ing changes in the conventional basis of valuation a short time ahead of the general public.[38]

The prevalence of "speculation" over "enterprise"—the forecasting of the prospective yield of an investment over its whole useful life—is a natural consequence of the function of Stock Exchanges which are organized to make investment as liquid as possible. The only way to mitigate the potential damage would thus be to make speculation more costly (e.g., by imposing a tax on the transfer of shares). The fact remains, however, that the ability to liquidate wealth-claims at any moment is essential to improve incentives to savers to buy shares representing existing capital goods. The accumulation mechanism based on autonomous decisions concerning real and financial accumulation suffers from an ambivalence which is hard to remove. The ideal would be a stock market that valued an investment in terms of its yield over its whole useful life, though to attain this it would be necessary "to make the purchase of an investment permanent and indissoluble like a marriage." Conversely, the Stock Exchange must be free to insure the liquidity of investment in shares, a freedom that procreates speculative activities that often transmit confusing or misleading signals about the yield on existing investment, thereby distorting the informational base available to entrepreneurs contemplating programs of new investment.

Seeping through the filter of the entrepreneur's state of mind, the information extracted from the Stock Exchange nonetheless contributes to the formation of the state of long-term expectations. At this phase in the decision-making process, "human logic" returns to the forefront: "Most, probably, of our decisions to do something positive, the full consequences of which will be drawn out over many days to come, can only be taken as a result of animal spirits."[39] Innately, it is these "animal spirits" which induce the entrepreneur to transcend cold calculations based on costs and returns and the probability of these matching his expectations.

It is the presence of these "animal spirits" which marks out the capitalist-entrepreneur, on whose entrepreneurial spirit capital accumulation and the stability of the system depends. "Confidence"

38. Ibid., p. 154.
39. Ibid., p. 161.

and the climate of opinion take hold, for states of mind are notoriously subject to waves of optimism and pessimism, so that emotional factors are capable of disrupting the existing flow in the economy, making investment not only more unstable but fragile.[40] This does not mean that investment must be subject to continuous violent upheavals, but it does mean that the continuous growth of capital over the long haul is only possible under a whole series of favorable circumstances.

40. In recent years, and particularly with respect to the financial institutional structure, this aspect has been frequently underscored by Hyman P. Minksy. See, e.g., Minsky, *John Maynard Keynes* (New York: Columbia University Press, 1975); and ibid., "An Economics of Keynes' Perspective on Money," in *Modern Economic Thought*, ed. Weintraub (Philadelphia: University of Pennsylvania Press, 1977).

CHAPTER 9

THE GENERAL THEORY: THE CHARACTERISTICS OF A MONETARY ECONOMY

During the period Keynes was preparing the *General Theory*, after having abandoned the viewpoint of the *Treatise*, he took the opportunity in a short essay in honor of Arthur Spiethoff to give a summary of his fresh thinking on the role of money.[1] He had already revised the title of his Cambridge lecture course from "The Pure Theory of Money" to "The Monetary Theory of Production," detailing the role of money in determining economic activity. The Spiethoff essay indicates the direction of his thought. His main objective was to discard the analytical strand which viewed money as "a neutral link between transactions in real things and real assets and does not allow it to enter into motives or decisions" (p. 408), as in the works of Marshall and Pigou where money plays a purely symbolic part and the system functions as in a barter economy and excludes money from crises or instability. Yet crises and instability appear precisely in monetary economies in which money exerts its potency on decisions to spend and on financial options. Previously, in the *Treatise*, Keynes had moved beyond the concept that money is in some way "neutral" and that variations in the quantity of money cannot affect real variables. Now, in this essay, he sought to approach capitalist reality more keenly in a theoretical schema capable of incorporating the fact that money modifies behavioral functions:

> The theory which I desiderate would deal, in contradistinction to this, with an economy in which money plays a part of its own and

---

1. Keynes, "A Monetary Theory of Production," *Festschrift für Arthur Spiethoff* (1933); reprinted in *C.W.K.*, vol. 13.

effects motives and decisions and is, in short, one of the operative factors in the situation, so that the course of events cannot be predicted, either in the long period or in the short, without a knowledge of the behavior of money between the first state and the last. And it is that which we ought to mean when we speak of a *monetary economy*. (Pp. 408–9)

If we bear this objective in Keynes's program in mind while reading the chapters on money in the *General Theory*, the significance of liquidity preference, the conventional nature of the interest rate, and the instability of the speculative demand for money become fully transparent. Above all, however, we can grasp the tie, ignored by most of the literature on Keynes, between liquidity preference and the marginal efficiency of capital, or the demand function for money and the demand function for investment.

There is clearly a more trivial link between the two functions operating via the influence that the money market interest rate exerts on investment. There also exists a second more fundamental link striking at the two functions' very existence and their significance in a capitalist "monetary economy," characterized by the separation between the earning of income and decisions to spend, and the instability of the value of assets. Both characteristics are subsumed by the presence of uncertainty. It is uncertainty which dominates investment decisions and displaces the classical identification of the capital accumulation process with the amassment of savings. Keynes substitutes a behavioral function in which "animal spirits" are the driving force. At the same time, however, uncertainty about the future compels individuals to seek a "liquid" shelter thereby underpinning a demand function for money.

For Keynes the interest rate is the "reward for parting with liquidity," or to be more precise, "the price which equilibrates the desire to hold wealth in the form of cash with the available quantity of cash."[2] It follows that the propensity to save, which traditional theory held as determining interest rates, has only a very limited role in deciding this particular price. Once a certain volume of savings is decided what really counts is the form of financial assets in which the savings are held. If all savings were retained in money the saver would not receive any interest at all. Thus "the rate of interest cannot be a return to saving or waiting as such."

2. *The General Theory*, in *C.W.K.* 7:167.

The quantity of money in the system reflects the behavior of the banking system and the monetary policy adopted by the central bank. As a first approximation, taking the behavior of the banking system as given, deferring its analysis to a later stage, and thus positing the stock of money supplied to the system as the fruit of autonomous decisions by the monetary authorities, the most immediate determinant of the interest rate is centered on liquidity preference. The pivotal query is: Why, to what extent, and as a function of what variables does the public hold a proportion of its wealth in coin, circulating banknotes, and current bank accounts?[3] The reply ultimately has to explain why money is held though the possessor receives no interest.

Keynes's broad reconsideration of the quantity theory in the *Treatise* armed him with a fairly precise answer about some of the motives that are conducive to the holding of liquid reserves. The individual needs an adequate quantity of money to protect himself against the inevitable lack of synchronization between receipts and payments: Keynes terms this the "transactions-motive," originating largely in the length of the period, or time discrepancy, between receipts and payments and depending on the level of income.

The "precautionary-motive" is another reason for holding liquid money. This derives from an "insurance" aspect, as a protection against a sudden need for money to meet unexpected outlay contingencies. Here, too, the size of the reserves varies with income.

Interest rates also exert some influence over the volume of funds held because of these motives, for they make the decisions on holding money instead of interest-bearing assets more, or less, costly. The income effect, however, is predominant.[4] The velocity of money—defined as the ratio (V) between income (Y) and the total quantity of money held to satisfy the transactions and the precautionary motive (M_1)—can be regarded as being "relatively" stable.

---

3. Keynes suggests that it is somewhat arbitrary to distinguish liquid reserves from credit, for the demarcation line consists simply in the length of the period within which it is possible to liquidate a credit if this is to be regarded as money.

4. Keynes works on the surmise that, at least in the short term, the interval between receipts and payments is constant. In practice, this is shorthand for the hypothesis that there are no changes in the banking structure, in industrial organization, or in public habits during the period under analysis.

Thus: $L_1(Y) = (Y/V) = M_1$, where $L_1(Y)$ stands for the functional relationship between the desired quantity of money for the motives listed and the level of income.

There also exists a pronounced financial motive for holding money, namely, uncertainty about the future course of interest rates. Traditional analysis has always neglected the underlying cause of this motive and indeed has simply overlooked the motive itself. Nonetheless, there are two separate yet closely interacting ways in which financial market uncertainty affects the demand for money. In the first place, if we do not know future interest rates, uncertainty surrounds the future value of a bond issued today and due to expire on a definite future date. Hence if the bond-owner needs cash and has to sell the bond in the interim before redemption there is the risk of a capital loss. With his having only a vague idea about future interest rates and a latent fear of a rise in rates, the uncertainty will encourage the building of liquid reserves: this provides ample explanation of why an adequate price has to be paid to encourage savers to sacrifice liquidity. It follows that a high interest rate—with an implicit promise of *lower* future rates—leads lenders to undertake greater purchases of bonds, thereby reducing the amount of cash held.

The relation between desired liquid reserves and the current rate of interest also asserts itself in another way, giving extra sustenance to Keynes's definition of this component in the total demand for money as the "speculative motive." A speculator in bonds always hopes to profit from a positive gap between their future and their current price. If then there is a belief that future rates of interest will be below current rates, money will be relinquished to acquire bonds. If the opposite opinion prevails, more money will be preferred: "The market price will be fixed at the point at which the sales of the 'bears' and the purchase of the 'bulls' are balanced."[5]

Is it possible to establish a relationship between the speculative demand for money and the current rate of interest? On the logic underlying speculation, demand for liquid reserves is a function of the gap between the present rate of interest and the rate that people tend to think is subsequently going to prevail. Keynes supposes that expectations about the future rate are independent of the current rate: it follows that the higher the current rate the

5. Ibid., p. 170.

more widely it will be expected that it is already above the expected rate and that in the future it will be lower. Keynes thus derives an inverse relationship between the speculative demand for money and the current rate of interest, thereby fortifying the negative relationship between the two variables.[6]

Denoting M_2 as the quantity of money held for speculative reasons and $L_2(r)$ as the demand function for liquid reserves for this motive, where r is the current rate of interest, equilibrium between total demand and total quantity of money M must satisfy the condition:

$$M = M_1 + M_2 = L_1(Y) + L_2(r).$$

Assuming that the speculative demand schedule can be aggregated from the behavior of individuals each of whom is motivated to act according to his own expectations of future rates, Keynes considers L_2 as a (continuous) falling function of r. It is through this channel that the effects of a manipulation in the quantity of money are transmitted to the economic system. An increase in the quantity of money, for example, through open market operations, presses on r, tending to stimulate investment. This, in its turn, produces, via the working of the multiplier, an increase in Y. Equilibrium is reestablished when M_2 and M_1 have risen sufficiently to absorb the new higher level of M. The size of the increase in M_2, as compared to that in M_1, depends on the elasticity of the speculative demand; for a given elasticity the degree to which monetary policy affects employment depends, according to Keynes, "on the responses of investment to a reduction in the rate of interest and of income to an increase in investment."[7] The vexing problem, however, is that the speculative demand for money, derived as it is from the efforts of individuals and firms to defend themselves against uncertainty, is a highly unstable function. The same considerations about the state of expectations, as discussed in chapter 8, thus apply with the only difference being that the object of speculation is the rate of interest estimated for some date in the future.[8]

---

6. Keynes emphasizes long-term bonds which are most sensitive to interest rate variations.

7. Ibid., p. 201.

8. To be more precise, the complex of rates of interest for assets due to fall due on different dates.

This instability holds as a corollary that there is absolutely no guarantee that an expansionary monetary policy will automatically depress interest rates. If, for example, the public is convinced that the rate of interest is going to be led upward, moving closer, say, to an international rate, then an increase in the money supply by the central bank will be interpreted as a purely temporary act and the extra money will be absorbed at a virtually unchanged rate. Essentially, there will be a rightward shift in the speculative demand schedule for money. A similar phenomenon will occur if the current interest rate is so low as to make any further reduction seem virtually impossible so that liquidity preference becomes "absolute" (what Robertson called the "liquidity trap"). Keynes thus concludes that the interest rate is a "highly conventional" phenomenon:

> It might be more accurate, perhaps, to say the rate of interest is a highly conventional, rather than a highly psychological, phenomenon. For its actual value is largely governed by the prevailing view as to what its value is expected to be. Any level of interest which is accepted with sufficient conviction as *likely* to be durable *will* be durable; subject, of course, in a changing society to fluctuations for all kinds of reasons round the expected normal.[9]

Considering the primitive characteristics that mark a monetary economy, Keynes ponders why economists' attention has always been riveted on the money rate of interest rather than the rate prevailing on loans of some other commodity. In raising this question he was reverting back to the contrast between a monetary and a nonmonetary economy which had emerged from Sraffa's contribution in the debate with Hayek.[10] Sraffa, it will be recalled, had argued that *every* commodity has a rate of interest in terms of itself (the "own rate" in Keynes's terminology), and equal to the rate of interest on loans in money plus the discrepancy between the current and the expected price for the commodity. Generally speaking, although each commodity has its "own rate," this would not prevent us from isolating any one of them for use as a unit of measurement. Theoretically, it would be possible to calculate the marginal efficiency of capital—the strategic magnitude for Keynes—using any commodity as standard. If the terms of trade among alternative standards remain constant—and there is no reason to consider these

9. Ibid., p. 203.
10. Keynes refers to Sraffa's article in a note to chap. 17.

as varying when we are simply discussing the choice of such a unit—then the marginal efficiency of capital will be the same when measured in money as when measured in wheat. Keynes concludes: "So far, therefore, the money-rate of interest has no uniqueness compared with other rates of interest but is on precisely the same footing."[11]

In analyzing the attributes that determine the interest rate for a capital good, three separate contributory factors can be identified: (1) the income (or net product) that investment goods produce when applied in the productive process, or the services that consumer durables yield to the consumer; (2) carrying (or maintenance) costs regardless of whether the particular capital good is actually used; (3) a liquidity premium which is a function of the ease of transforming the capital asset in question into liquid assets. The "rate of return" on any durable asset is the algebraic sum of the values of these three attributes (carrying costs are negative).

The characteristic of investment goods and consumer durables is that their net return exceeds their maintenance cost and they have negligible liquidity premium. Unused investment goods (and inventories) yield nil income. As their maintenance cost is usually above their liquidity premium, their actual return is thus negative. Money produces no income but at the same time involves practically nil maintenance charges[12] and a high liquidity premium.

Once these different rates of return are expressed in terms of a given commodity chosen as the standard (let us suppose it is money) wealth owners will seek out those assets with the highest rates of return, thereby creating a market price system for capital goods which irons out the divergent "own rates": "Thus in equilibrium the demand-prices of houses and wheat in terms of money will be such that there is nothing to choose in the way of advantage between the alternatives."[13] Essentially, for each of the goods, and for money itself, the rate of money return will tend to be equalized.[14]

This equilibrating leveling of returns affects the composition

---

11. *General Theory*, in *C.W.K.* 7:225.

12. Other than some minor charges in provision against theft, or charges for a safe deposit box, etc.

13. Ibid., pp. 227–28.

14. If one takes account of the different risk attached to each asset as well as of their return, one sees that Keynes's equality of returns is completely compatible with the characteristic inequality in the modern portfolio equilibrium.

of wealth. Side by side, there is a parallel process involving the production flow of new capital goods, that is, of investment. Out of the expectational framework and "animal spirits," and bearing in mind the shadow cast by the supply price of capital goods, the marginal efficiency of certain capital goods may surpass the rate of return on the corresponding capital goods already in existence, thus underwriting a demand for their production. As investment in each particular good increases, its marginal efficiency falls. How much will be invested and how much produced, as a consequence, of each particular kind of capital?

Keynes had already shown that a floor for the fall in the marginal efficiency of capital is laid by the rate of interest on loans in money. Now he observes that in theory the limit inheres in the asset's rate of interest which "declines most slowly as the stock of assets in general increases." Therefore, the only warrant for the choice of the money rate is that this is the interest rate which is most reluctant to fall:

> If by *money* we mean the standard of value, it is clear that it is not necessarily the money-rate of interest which makes the trouble. We could not get out of our difficulties (as some have supposed) merely by decreeing that wheat or houses shall be the standard of value instead of gold or sterling. For, it now appears that the same difficulties will ensue if there continues to exist *any* asset of which the own-rate of return is reluctant to decline as output increases. [15]

Manifestly, there are revealed certain unsettling characteristics of a monetary economy which make money the asset whose rate of return is most reluctant to fall. First there is the fact of an almost total inelasticity of the production of money. [16] In a system of paper money, private citizens cannot increase the production of money regardless of the rise in its value; even in a gold standard system the prospect of augmenting money supply is limited by the productive efficiency of existing gold mines. Recognizing that a like inelasticity of supply is common to other rent-bearing capital goods, it is

---

15. *General Theory*, in *C.W.K.* 7:229.

16. Paul Davidson has recently emphasized this in "The Dual-Faceted Nature of the Keynesian Revolution: Money and Money Wages in Unemployment and Production Flow Prices," *Journal of Post-Keynesian Economics*, Fall 1980.

incumbent to stipulate the peculiarity of the money rate of return. A second characteristic of money is that its elasticity of substitution for other assets is extremely low. Even if the price level rises, reducing the value of money in terms of goods, this does not enable us to substitute money for other productive agents. But if variations are expected in the future value of money, there may well be changes in the desired composition of wealth, with a trend for financial assets to be substituted for real assets, thereby tending to equalize the "own-rates" of interest in the way considered earlier.

A third fundamental element resides in the ability of money to satisfy the need for liquidity; there is a floor interest rate at which the public will be willing to absorb any quantity of money, thereby blocking any further decline in the rate.

One escape-hatch to this fixity in the supply of money could emanate from a fall in money wages, which, because of a reduced transactions demand would be equivalent to an increased money quantity. Much has been made of this possibility in several interpretations of the *General Theory*;[17] it was not excluded in principle by Keynes. Keynes believed, however, that it was equally plausible that a fall in money wages would drag down the marginal efficiency of capital. What counts in braking investment is the relative downward rigidity of the rate of interest as compared to the marginal efficiency of capital; a fall in money wages does not modify Keynes's conclusions over the rigidity in the money supply. Ultimately, the only serious way to reduce money rates of interest, permitting a further fall in capital goods' "own-rates" and fostering investment, is for the monetary authorities to augment the money supply. In a nonmoney economy where no other commodity had the peculiar properties of money, competition would tend to press down the rate of return on individual assets "until the emergence of full employment had brought about for commodities generally the inelasticity of supply which we have postulated as a normal characteristic of money."[18]

Keynes's conclusion is thus that in the absence of money the system would tend spontaneously toward full employment, whereas in the presence of money the equilibrium will normally settle at

17. See in particular, F. Modigliani, "Liquidity Preference and the Theory of Interest and Money," *Econometrica* (1944), pp. 45–88.
18. *General Theory*, in *C.W.K.* 7:235.

underemployment. If full employment is to be realized more money is necessary.

The argument confirms that it is money that underlies both the liquidity preference and the investment demand function. To state that in the absence of money the investment stream would stretch sufficiently to facilitate full employment is tantamount to saying that investment *automatically* balances the full employment savings, that is, there exists *no* independent investment demand function. The analytical need to express entrepreneurs' decisions to invest through an investment function derives from the presence of money in an economy characterized by uncertainty. With uncertainty and money, it becomes an imperative to accept the fact of a liquidity preference schedule. Hayek had argued that the quantity of money ought to be held constant so as to duplicate the spontaneous equilibrium characteristics of a nonmonetary economy. Keynes's analysis, on the other hand, dissents wholeheartedly: for an uncertain and monetized economy his judgment is that a constant money supply would prevent the system from reaching full employment. An increased supply of money is not, however, a sufficient condition to alleviate unemployment.

The particular significance of the money rate of interest transcends the choice of money as a unit of value, but Keynes remarks that the characteristics of money are made more perceptible by the fact that debts and wages are stipulated in terms of money. Money's high liquidity premium is to a great extent due to the fact that

> contracts are fixed, and wages are usually somewhat stable, in terms of money. . . . The convenience of holding assets in the same standard as that in which future liabilities may fall due and in a standard in terms of which the future cost of living is expected to be relatively stable, is obvious. At the same time the expectation of relative stability in the future money-cost of output might not be entertained with much confidence if the standard of value were a commodity with a high elasticity of production.[19]

Nevertheless, Keynes alleges that the expectation that future money costs of production will be relatively stable is attributable

---

19. Ibid., pp. 236–37.

not so much to the fact that wages are fixed in money as to the fact that money wages are "sticky." Conceivably, there may be a commodity other than money in terms of which wages would be even more sticky, more stable. Its cost of production would have to be constant, and to stock it would have to be largely cost-free as soon as production outran current demand. In practice, however, it is extremely unlikely that we could find such a good for which the discrepancy between the liquidity premium and the carrying cost is higher than for money. As a result the various characteristics that insure that money's "own-rate" of interest is most important for the system tend to interreact:

> The fact that money has low elasticities of production and substitution and low carrying-costs tends to raise the expectation that money-wages will be relatively stable; and this expectation enhances money's liquidity-premium and prevents the exceptional correlation between the money-rate of interest and the marginal efficiencies of other assets which might, if it could exist, rob the money-rate of interest of its sting.[20]

Keynes thus sees the stickiness of money wages as an added peculiar trait of a monetary economy, and he assigns this stickiness as a primary factor for stability within the system. When money wages are constant it is mainly effective demand which perturbs prices, real wages, and employment as output adapts to the altered effective demand. If, on the other hand, as argued by Pigou,[21] for example, it is real wages that tend to be stable, then any fall in effective demand would reduce prices and money wages while employment and output remained steadfast. There would, however, still be an excess supply of goods, a further fall in prices and wages, and so on. Relatively stable employment would thus be accompanied by extremely unstable prices. Reflecting on the concrete experience of the 1930s, Keynes deemed this theoretical hypothesis unrealistic; reality confirmed that employment variations prevailed.

It is on the joint effects of variations in money wages and prices

---

20. Ibid., p. 238.
21. A. C. Pigou, *The Theory of Unemployment* (London: Macmillan, 1933).

that Keynes concentrates his attention once he completes building his skeletal theoretical structure.[22]

Before examining these aspects of the *General Theory* in detail, it is worth reviewing briefly his whole schema and reiterating its fundamental analytic blocks.[23] Aggregate demand from households, firms, government, and the outside world is obviously the motor driving income and production: according to Keynes's "law of the marginal propensity to consume," a dollar of income generates less than a dollar of consumption. This implies, therefore, that the only way of guaranteeing equilibrium between aggregate demand and supply is through filling the income-consumption gap through an adequate amount of autonomous expenditure. Apart from public expenditure and exports, assumed at a first approximation to be exogenous, it is thus investment that would determine the level of activity at which the system operates. The investment volume depends on the combined effect of "the physical conditions of supply in the capital-goods industries, the state of confidence concerning the prospective yield, the psychological attitude to liquidity and the quantity of money."[24]

The relation between the volume of investment (and of the other autonomous components of expenditure, namely, govern-

22. Keynes's analysis is targeted on the effects of variations in money wages. Despite the crucial importance assigned to the fact that the wage bargain is in money terms, Keynes offers no theory of money wage determination. This problem has been the focus of Sidney Weintraub's macrotheory since at least 1958: "economic analysis lacks a theory of *money* wages. . . . A more serious start will have to be made to construct a version that embraces the historical, social, and political forces impelling money wages" (Weintraub, "The Missing Theory of Money Wages," *Journal of Post-Keynesian Economics*, Winter 1978–79).

23. For the same reasons that restrained Keynes, it appeared to me as inopportune to translate the logical schema of the *General Theory* into a formal model. As he put it: "I am more attached to the comparatively simple fundamental ideas which underlie my theory than to the particular forms in which I have embodied them, and I have no desire that the latter should be crystallised at the present stage of the debate. If the simple basic ideas can become familiar and acceptable, time and experience and the collaboration of a number of minds will discover the best way of expressing them" ("The General Theory of Employment," *The Quarterly Journal of Economics* [February 1937], pp. 211–12).

24. Keynes, *General Theory*, in *C.W.K.* 7:248.

ment outlay and exports) and income is given by the multiplier: its value is positively related to the marginal propensity to consume and negatively influenced by the "marginal propensity to import." Assuming equality between investment and employment multiplier, then output and employment are bound together in a tight mesh. Exogenous increases in one of the components of aggregate demand are thus conducive to magnified jumps in output and employment. With an unchanged money supply the income advance will occasion an increased transactions demand for money and some uptick in interest rates. In equilibrium, investment is thus somewhat suppressed compared to its extent if the money supply responded positively to a higher activity level.

The *General Theory* thus crystallizes as a system of interconnected propositions erected on a substructure of a number of given elements: the existing productive plant, technology, the degree of competition, consumer habits, the disutility of labor, and the distribution of income. Keynes's specific functional parameters or "ultimate independent variables" consist of the propensity to consume, the nature of liquidity preference, the expected yield from capital goods, the level of money wages, and the money supply. The two variables whose determination constitutes the objective of the whole analysis are national income and the level of employment.

Any variation in the assumed given elements, or in the exogenously determined magnitudes, would affect the endogenous magnitudes. Above all, however—and this is the key aspect in Keynes's vision of the capitalist market system—some of the parameters of the system, especially those tied to investment and liquidity expectations, could well bounce around arbitrarily and with ease: "Thus the position of equilibrium will be influenced by these repercussions; and there are other repercussions also. Moreover, there is not one of the above factors which is not liable to change without much warning, and sometimes substantially. Hence the extreme complexity of the actual course of events."[25]

Money wages and prices were central to Keynes's system of magnitudinal money propositions.[26] As for wages, a critical ques-

---

25. Ibid., p. 249.

26. Cf. Weintraub, *Capitalism, Inflation and Unemployment Crisis,* chaps. 3 and 5.

tion concerned their effect on employment if these fell: a reduction in wages was the commonplace prescription in the 1930s to alleviate the depression. Unemployment caused by downward rigidity of money wages was a proposition proffered by orthodox economics as fully compatible with the traditional theory: as noted earlier, the classical theory claimed that full employment was attainable through general cuts in money wages. Implicit in the argument was the hypothesis that more output through higher employment would lead to a corresponding increase in demand (via Say's Law). Keynes rejected this traditional conclusion, arguing that it confused supply and demand curves for a single industry, based on the underlying "constant" income hypothesis, with aggregate curves and illegitimately transferred the concepts to the whole economy. The classical theory assumed that a fall in wages would engender a rightward shift in the supply curve, and a new equilibrium at a lower level of prices and higher output and employment. Oddly, the implicit demand curves would remain immobile despite the income drop in money wages.[27]

In the model presented in the *General Theory*, a fall in money wages will increase employment only if aggregate money demand holds firm, or declines by less than the fall in money wages, thus signifying an aggregate demand increase as measured in wage units. Keynes reiterates that aggregate demand—in wage units—rests on the consumption function, the marginal efficiency of capital schedule, and the interest rate. Therefore the channel by which a reduction in money wages can enhance employment would necessarily have to be based on one of these factors. He then goes on to consider the various possible ways in which these factors may change in a direction favorable or unfavorable to employment after a money wage decline. The analysis is a fascinating sample of Keynes's *un*dogmatic approach compared to later interpretations of his work, which were far more doctrinaire and simplistic.[28]

---

27. Cf. Weintraub, *Approach to the Theory of Income*, chaps. 1 and 8, where the traditional theory, and Keynes's contention, are treated diagrammatically.

28. The influential interpretations of J. R. Hicks ("Mr. Keynes and the 'Classics': A Suggested Interpretation," *Econometrica*, January 1937); Modigliani ("Liquidity Preference"); and L. Klein (*The Keynesian Revolution* [New York: Macmillan, 1949]), which formed the skeleton of the

1. As a consequence of lower prices ensuing from the wage fall, there would be a redistribution of income to those whose remuneration remained relatively constant, and thus in favor of rentiers. The result: presumably a higher propensity to save with negative employment effects.

2. Assuming foreign wages constant, there would be a better export competitivity, and thus an improvement in the balance of trade. Positive job prospects would be contingent on the economy's international "openness."

3. There would be some worsening in the terms of trade and a consequent fall in real incomes. Some ensuing enlargement in the propensity to consume could exert a favorable effect on employment.

4. Price deflation would heighten the debt burden, increase the possibility of bankruptcies and thus create a climate of pessimism that would not be conducive to investment.

5. The marginal efficiency of capital could go either way, depending on whether prevailing opinion believes that the current fall in wages is a prelude to a subsequent increase or to further declines.

6. There would be a downward drift in the transactions demand for money, equivalent to an augmented money supply, as measured in real terms (or wage units). This would be conducive to lower interest rates. If expectations incline to an upswing in the marginal efficiency of capital, because of forecasts on higher future prices, this favorable employment aspect would be jeopardized.

Expectations of this sort, however, are intermingled with expectations of higher interest rate phenomena which could touch off a speculative demand for money. Likewise, this market infringement could follow if wage reductions upset public confidence or provoke a deterioration in the general political climate.

Keynes concludes, after this exemplary and thorough survey, that if one excludes the influence of a "beggar my neighbor" foreign trade improvement, anyone who places faith in the expansionary virtues of a money wage reduction must base his hopes on a drop in interest rates. Here, however, one finds all the same difficulties

---

Keynesian paradigm, saw the reductions in money wages as tantamount to an increase in money supply, thereby tending to increase real incomes and jobs.

inherent in policies aimed at increasing the money supply whose consequences can be overshadowed by aberrations or instability in liquidity preference.

Any reasonable analysis would recognize the practical impossibility of accomplishing a nearly uniform reduction of wages: a struggle between different sectors of the economy, and various labor groups, would occur. Recognizing, too, the income shift to rentiers through the existence of fixed money incomes, wage cuts undoubtedly would be about the least advisable of the two policies, that is, keeping money wages constant and increasing the money supply or keeping the money supply constant and reducing money wages. Moreover one has also to consider the possible adverse effects on the marginal efficiency of capital and the extra deflationary burden of a debt magnified by price reductions.

What of the movement of the price level? The *General Theory* has often been conveyed in the form of a "fix-price" model. Actually the *General Theory*, unlike the *Treatise*, contains relatively little *explicit* analysis of the process wherein relative prices are formed, even at the minimal level of disaggregation needed to distinguish prices of consumer and capital goods. Keynes does provide, however, a definite perspective on the general price level. With given money wages, equilibrium prices depend on the tie between effective demand, the output level, and employment; prices are immanent in his theory. The equilibrium price level for a given effective demand entails a real wage, and so a demand for labor, sufficient to balance production and aggregate demand.

Keynes, in his chapter 21, "The Theory of Prices," opens by contesting the traditional dichotomy between the theory of value and distribution and the theory of money and prices. It was this compartmentalization which enabled the classical economists to regard the price level as a matter involving exclusively the interaction between money and prices, as in the Cambridge equation. Conversely, in Keynes's *General Theory* the quantity of money and the price level are fully incorporated within the methodological logic underlying a monetary economy. Thus for a given level of output the price level depends on money wages, via the latter's effect on marginal money costs. Premising diminishing marginal productivity—in emulation of the orthodox tradition—when productive capacity is given, variations in output perturb marginal costs at *given* money wages. The relation between money and prices is thus indirect: it first requires a direct examination of the effects of variations in the quantity of money on effective demand.

Greater union pressure and management acquiescence in pay raises during expansionary periods will usually increase wages even before full employment is achieved. Money wages (and "user-costs") will ordinarily rise even before full employment. The following quotation from Keynes is especially pertinent for its keen realism in the light of subsequent events:

> If there is a perfect balance in the respective quantities of specialised unemployed resources, the point of full employment will be reached for all of them simultaneously. But, in general, the demand for some services and commodities will reach a level beyond which their supply is, for the time being, perfectly inelastic, whilst in other directions there is still a substantial surplus of resources without employment. Thus as output increases, a series of "bottle-necks" will be successively reached, where the supply of particular commodities ceases to be elastic and their prices have to rise to whatever level is necessary to divert demand into other directions. (P. 300)

CHAPTER 10

KEYNES AND
THE CLASSICAL ECONOMISTS

From the beginning to the end of the *General Theory*, Keynes continually insisted on the break between his own theory and that of the classical economists. He was convinced that the operative forces in the capitalist system are incapable of promoting consistent full resource utilization or of creating conditions ensuring that the economy moves spontaneously toward its full employment stance. Unemployment is not to be discerned as a temporary phenomenon ascribable only to frictions or imperfections: it is a structural attribute of capitalism. Furthermore, the extreme instability in the marginal efficiency of capital and in liquidity preference precludes simplistic rules of economic policy capable of automatically steering the economy to the full employment goal. Keynes's challenge to the traditional theory can hardly be overstated.

Keynes's attack on the "classical" theory can be better understood by recalling the limitations encountered by the *Treatise's* attempted rupture of the dominant theory. Dissatisfied with his earlier failure, Keynes now took new strength from the belief that he had delivered the decisive blow to classical theory. But his confidence was not generally shared by his contemporaries, many of whom did not greet the *General Theory* warmly. More enduring issues concern later generations: was Keynes's message a transitory or a truly original step in economic thought? In seeking an answer to this question, it will be necessary to skate around what has become an enormous interpretative literature, in many languages.

The principal target of critics of the *General Theory*, and the main test of its validity as a theoretical analysis of the capitalist system, was Keynes's attack on the "classical economists"—the term he applied to his predecessors, without exception. To understand the significance of Keynes's charge, it will help to examine his attack in greater depth. As already noted, Keynes believed that the classical economists had based the two full employment postulates on one proposition, namely, Say's Law, or the idea that investment always automatically balances full employment savings. As he remarked, this thought of Ricardo "conquered England as completely as the Holy Inquisition conquered Spain."

In the Hayek debate, Keynes lumped the investment theory of the new Austrian monetary school with traditional theory,[1] rejecting it precisely on the ground of his vision of how capital accumulation works in practice. Hence if it was unacceptable to assume that investment automatically adapts to the level of savings necessary to insure full employment, it follows that in the *General Theory* he had to show that the classical equality between savings and investment is actually an identity obtained through the assumption of investment being a variable instead of an independent function. In any assessment of the theoretical novelty of the *General Theory*, this is a cardinal point. In the interpretative literature since Hicks,[2] investment is widely acknowledged to be a function of the interest rate also in the classical theory.

There exists, then, a problem in interpreting the classical theory of investment or at least in interpreting the way the *General Theory* identifies it. Without clarity on this point it is impossible to understand the significance and range of Keynes's assault on the theory of the interest rate. In chapter 2 Keynes warns that the theory of an equilibrium between savings and investment was no longer formulated as explicitly by the classical school as it was by Ricardo and Say. In chapter 14, however, in which he reviews the classical theory, he assumes both savings and investment as functions of the interest rate:

> It is fairly clear, however, that this tradition has regarded the rate of interest as the factor which brings the demand for investment and the willingness to save into equilibrium with one another. Investment represents the demand for investible resources and saving rep-

---

1. In the *General Theory* Keynes tends to use neoclassical as an adjective for the school that inspired Hayek's theories (*General Theory*, in *C.W.K.* 7:183).
2. "Mr. Keynes and the 'Classics.'"

resents the supply, whilst the rate of interest is the "price" of investible resources at which the two are equated. (P. 175)

It is not easy to explain this changed conception in which Keynes tended to associate the classical theory of investment with approximately his own schedule of the marginal efficiency of capital. More obscure is the reason why in the same chapter 14 he charges the classical theory of interest with "formal error." After he outfitted the classical theory with an investment demand function, the only criticism that seems warranted on the *General Theory*'s reasoning is that of having neglected the dependency of savings on income and, of course, of having entirely overlooked liquidity preference.

In the summer of 1935 Keynes sent Roy F. Harrod a copy of the early proofs for the *General Theory*. In ensuing correspondence, chapter 14 was the one most strongly criticized by his former pupil. Comparing the final version with earlier drafts, this also appears to be the chapter that gave Keynes the most trouble.[3]

Harrod protested that in accusing the classical economists, and Marshall in particular, of having promulgated a "senseless" theory of interest, Keynes was unjust.[4] To sustain his charge, Keynes argues that the interest rate cannot balance savings and investment because, in the classical view, these two magnitudes are always equal anyway. According to Harrod, Keynes was incorrect: that demand and supply magnitudes are always equal does not deny the existence of a price variable to bring them into balance. The defect in the classical theory was instead its neglect of the adjustment process between savings and investment whereby a third significant variable is invoked, namely, the level of income. For Harrod, indicting classical theory for error draws the reader off in the wrong direction and conceals Keynes's genuinely novel contribution to the theory of income determination. The classical theory is wrong, Harrod insists in a later letter, when it claims that an increase in the propensity to save reduces the interest rate.[5] This error, how-

---

3. An appendix to vol. 14 of the *C.W.K.* allows us to compare the first, second, and third proofs of the *General Theory* with the final version, and thus to see the modifications made by Keynes in his various drafts.

4. *C.W.K.* 13:530–32.

5. Ibid., p. 545.

ever, is nothing more than a logical consequence of the neglect of income as a determinant of savings, an omission that prevented the classical economists from visualizing the multiplier adjustment process.

In his rebuttal Keynes taunts Harrod with continuing to reason in concert with the classicists and reiterates his adamancy in proclaiming his break with their theory: "I *want*, so to speak, to raise a dust; because it is only out of the controversy that it will raise that what I am saying will get understood."[6] The argument invoked to support his view that the classical theory of interest is "nonsense" follows the script of the *General Theory*:

> The main point is, however, that my theory is essentially not a theory that the rate of interest is the factor which, allowing for changes in the level of income, brings the propensity to save into equilibrium with the inducement to invest. My theory is that the rate of interest is the price which brings the demand for liquidity into equilibrium with the amount of liquidity available. It has nothing whatever to do with saving.[7]

This reply to Harrod's objection appears unpersuasive. Harrod's point was that if one ignores liquidity preference and accepts the proposition that income is determined by the full employment condition, then the classical theory can determine the interest rate. The central point of debate remains the nature of the savings and investment equilibrium in the classical theory. Harrod reasons from $S(r,Y) = I(r)$, and it is difficult to deny that once Y has been determined so as to guarantee a level of employment which balances labor supply and demand this relation is sufficient to determine the equilibrium level of r. The classical economists can be faulted for not having detected liquidity preference, meaning the relation $M = L(Y,r)$; in Harrod's view this was Keynes's main contribution, for it entails that it is impossible to assume that income is independently driven to full employment. Nonetheless, on its own hypothesis the classical theory could not be assailed for logical incoherence.

Keynes's letter contains a postscript which reveals the essence of his original stance on the problem:

---

6. Ibid., p. 548.
7. Ibid., p. 550.

P.S. Will you ponder the following propositions:

1. Saving and investment are merely alternative names for the difference between income and consumption.

2. The supply curve of savings and the demand curve for investments have no determinate point of intersection, since they lie along one another in all conditions throughout the whole of their length. This applies equally in equilibrium or in disequilibrium. There are no conceivable circumstances in which the one curve does not occupy the same situation as the other throughout its length;—provided, of course, the same conditions, whatever conditions are assumed, are taken as applying to both alike.

3. The propensity to save and the schedule of marginal efficiencies are two curves which do not intersect anywhere, because they are not *in pari materia* and do not relate to the same variables. The propensity to save is a curve which relates the amount of savings to the amount of income. The schedule of the marginal efficiencies of capital is a curve which relates the amount of investment to the rate of interest. There is no sense in which they can be said to intersect.

What then remains? What are the demand and supply (other than those for liquidity) which the rate of interest is in certain hypothetical positions supposed to equilibrate?[8]

Although the previous line of argument is rather unfortunate, the postscript is directly tied to the view of the classical theory which Keynes had expressed in his discussion of employment. Now he is careful to distinguish the classical theory's "supply curve of savings" and "demand curve for investments" from his own schedules for the "propensity to save" and the "marginal efficiency of capital." The classical curves, as a consequence of Say's Law, according to which "supply creates its own demand," necessarily coincide so that they show an infinite set of values of S and I which correspond, when Y is fixed at full employment, to the infinite set of values of r in the relation $S(r,Y) = I$. Keynes's two curves correspond, on the other hand, to the $S(Y) = I(r)$ relation. Keynes did not exclude some influence of r on savings on a priori grounds, but in his view the latter was essentially determined by Y. This explains why he was insisting strongly that the two curves were not *in pari materia*.

In the final draft of chapter 14 this account of the issue is miss-

---

8. Ibid., pp. 552–53.

ing. Harrod had finally managed to convince Keynes that he had correctly understood the model proposed in the *General Theory*, and he suggested a graph to clarify his interpretation of the classical theory of interest.[9] Paradoxically, Keynes accepted this graph (the only one in the whole *General Theory*), attempting to turn it in defense of his own view. But the shift onto Harrod's ground serves to buttress—unintentionally—the latter's argument.[10]

The graph is nothing more nor less than a representation of the relation $S(r,Y) = I(r)$ for different levels of Y. Keynes posits a downward shift in the marginal efficiency of capital and observes that it is impossible to elicit the new equilibrium level of r, for the perturbation in the marginal efficiency of capital also causes an income tremor whose size cannot be established from the graph. Thus he concludes: "the functions used by the classical theory, namely, the response of investment and the response of the amount saved out of a given income to change in the rate of interest, do not furnish material for a theory of the rate of interest."[11] Not unexpectedly the graph could not serve any other purpose than that for which Harrod proposed it, namely, to prove that in ignoring liquidity preference, and by assuming that income is determined exogenously, any shift in the two schedules could be absorbed through variations in the rate of interest.

It is impossible to establish exactly the extent of Harrod's influence on Keynes's ultimate critique of the classical theory of interest. What does seem clear is that he gradually diverted his attention from Ricardo and Say, who took savings and investment as being substantially identical, to the more obscure "refinements" of Marshall, Cassel, and Pigou, whom he assigned to the same school. All of them did contend that the interest rate was determined through the interaction of the supply of savings and the demand for capital. Interestingly, in the most rigorous general equilibrium formulation of Leon Walras,[12] the interest rate is attached to the hypothesis that the economy will always absorb the production accruing from full factor utilization.

---

9. Ibid., pp. 553–56.
10. Ibid., pp. 557–59; *General Theory*, in *C.W.K.* 7:179–81.
11. *General Theory*, in *C.W.K.* 7:181.
12. *Elements of Pure Economics*.

In Walras's accumulation model the production of new capital goods is determined simultaneously with other quantity and price variables. Full factor utilization, involving an equilibrium between supply and demand for all existing kinds of productive services, is obtained by making the demand for one good a residual to absorb any remainder between income at full employment and the desired demand for all other goods.[13] In the aggregated model of Keynes, which limits itself to the distinction between consumer and investment goods, this connotes (in Walrasian terms) consumption or investment as endogenous magnitudes which urge production to full employment.

One of Walras's conditions is that savings and the production of new capital goods are always driven to equilibrium. Walras devotes an appendix of his book to this problem, setting the values of all the other variables in the model as given.[14] In this partial equilibrium analysis savings (as measured in the *numéraire*) and the value of newly produced capital goods (also in the *numéraire*) are equated. Both magnitudes are joined through the interest rate. Savings is a rising function (within a certain range) of the interest rate, which also determines the price of *each* capital good on an equilibrium footing equalizing the price of the good and the discounted value of its services. Walras is thus able to show graphically that the interest rate is determined at the intersection of the savings curve and a curve embodying the value of the new capital goods.

It is possible that this analytically rigorous general equilibrium[15] relation between savings and capital accumulation was the basis for the vague or even erroneous strictures Keynes refers to in chapter 14.[16] It is nonetheless strange that he puts Walras in the "classical

---

13. Ibid., Lesson 24.

14. Ibid., Appendix 1, pt. 3.

15. I leave aside here the determinacy and economic relevancy of the various solutions to Walras's model with respect to accumulation. In recent years these have prompted in Italy a vigorous debate with contributions by P. Garegnani, B. Trezza, A. Graziani, C. Napoleoni, D. Tosato, G. Di Nardi, and E. Zaghini. For a fuller bibliography see Zaghini, *L'accumulazione di capitale* (Rome: Edizioni Ateneo, 1967).

16. As recent criticism has demonstrated (see, for example, in Works Cited, Garegnani [1970], Spaventa, and Harcourt, who includes a critical summary), those theories which depend on a relation between "aggregate" capital and the interest rate are profoundly confused.

tradition."[17] He is correct in the sense that Walras ought to represent an essential reference point in any analysis of the "classical" school. Walras, in fact, offers the only rigorous formulation of the theory of the production of new capital goods that the "school" ever produced.

A careful examination of Walras (Lesson 24), however, would have alerted Keynes to try a different assault on the classical theory of interest, one which would have cleared the ground of all the ambiguities that mar chapter 14 of the *General Theory*. In the Walras schema, which assumes full factor utilization, the interest rate is determined *simultaneously* with all the other variables typical of a general equilibrium model lacking Keynes's principle of effective demand. The stylized version of the model, used by a number of classical economists (Marshall, Cassel, Pigou, Taussig), as well as by Harrod himself, is based on the relation $S(Y,r) = I(r)$, which incorporates the principle of effective demand implicit in the simultaneous treatment of a savings (and thus a consumption) function on the one hand, and an investment function on the other.

This version is, however, an incorrect synthesis of the classical theory and a recourse to Keynes's logical schema.[18] Given the logical connection between the marginal efficiency of capital and liquidity preference, it becomes imperative to inject the function $M = L(r,Y)$. Keynes, then, is right in insisting on liquidity preference to determine the r and Y. He should have stipulated, however, that without the notion of liquidity preference the savings and investment tangle becomes reduced to $S(Y,r) = I$. This would reflect a correct synthesis of classical theory; from this perspective it is correct to argue that the classical $S = I$ relation cannot validly establish the interest rate. When Keynes remarks that there is no substantial difference between the "marginal efficiency of capital" and the "demand curve for capital contemplated by some of the classical writers,"[19] the concession certainly does not help clarify the issue.

The fundamental misconception clouding the classical interest rate analysis is the failure to distinguish—as Walras does so cor-

17. *General Theory*, in *C.W.K.* 7:177.
18. Cf. Vicarelli, Introduzione, in *La controversia Keynesiana*, ed. Vicarelli (Bologna: Il Mulino, 1974).
19. *General Theory*, in *C.W.K.* 7:178.

rectly—between the demand for the productive services of the various factors (and thus for the various kinds of investment goods), and the absorption of new capital goods produced during the same period. In equilibrium it is the total value of this production flow which is equated to savings. The interest rate, on the other hand, ties the price of capital goods to the prices for their services. In the *General Theory* the urge of entrepreneurs to purchase the produced capital goods is vital to generating activity in the whole system; in Walras's model, an outlet for these goods is guaranteed by investment flexibility and the $S = I$ relation appears capable, on its own, of determining the interest rate without raising the vital problem of the compatibility of this model with effective demand. If Keynes had not been misled by appearances and had raised this question explicitly, as he did in a veiled way in his letter to Harrod, it would have been transparent—as he himself had insisted in the first part of the *General Theory*—that the key difference which divided him from the classicists was *effective demand*. This could only be incorporated into the classical framework by abandoning one of the theory's other equilibrium (or behavioral) relations.[20]

The contrast between the *General Theory* and traditional theory was starkly apparent to the generation of young economists of the 1930s. Educated in the classical themes, they reacted as if rebuked by Keynes for having swallowed theoretical propositions which were contradicted by reality, or missed out in logical coherence. It was hardly surprising that many sought to save some of the "credo" acquired so recently and at studious pain. Noteworthy was the review of the *General Theory* by R. F. Harrod, who undertook to extract those of Keynes's propositions "that are in conflict with the theory of value in the form in which it has hitherto been commonly accepted by most economists."[21] Harrod's general attitude toward Keynes's work fairly reflected the opinions crystallized in the 1935 correspondence. What Harrod sought to separate was Keynes's contribution to the general equilibrium model and the inherent

20. Cf. Vicarelli, Introduzione; cf. also M. Morishima, "Leon Walras and Money," and *Walras' Economics* (Cambridge: At the University Press, 1977).

21. Harrod, "Mr. Keynes and the Traditional Theory," *Econometrica* (January 1937), p. 74.

novelty of certain of his propositions elected from partial equilibrium analysis. In the former respect Keynes, in Harrod's view, merely readjusted various elements in the traditional theory. On the other hand, his scalpel changed significantly many aspects of partial equilibrium analysis, with important practical policy consequences.

Harrod regards the interest rate as a significant basis for comparing Keynes's and the traditional theory. The traditional theory, in Harrod's interpretation, yields the interest rate as the fulcrum for the capital demand and the supply of savings functions while imputing income as a datum. The investment function of the *General Theory* is mainly indistinguishable from the comparable function of classical theory: "The marginal productivity of capital appears in Mr. Keynes' book under the title of marginal efficiency."[22] Similarly, the two savings functions merged, with the significant addendum: Keynes's function includes income among the explicit variables, thereby rendering the *coeteris paribus* hypothesis, imposed by traditional theory, most unnecessary.

Harrod recognized that by tying interest rates to the market for money, Keynes succeeded in disintegrating the dichotomous wall between value and monetary theory typical of the classicists. Harrod's review, however, carried only a faint echo of the vast and intricate issues raised by the *General Theory*. His identification of marginal efficiency with the marginal productivity of capital exhibits a failure to appreciate the role of uncertainty and expectations, a major and original feature of Keynes's model. By seizing only on liquidity preference he missed the significance of expectations in the dynamic motion of a monetary economy, which was Keynes's key vision. In a very polite letter,[23] Keynes commented that he was content with the review, but called Harrod's attention to two matters. First was the differing attitudes of his own generation versus those of the younger economists in the debate with the traditional theory. For the former there was no way of revising their attitude, which was anchored in the past. The latter, on the other hand, have no consolidated theory of their own, and completely evade the ob-

---

22. Ibid., p. 76. For Harrod, Keynes's emphasis on the role of expectations was important and constitutes "a great improvement in the definition of marginal productivity," but "might be incorporated in traditional theory without entailing important modifications in its other parts."

23. *C.W.K.* 14:84–86.

stacles to be overcome: "The particles of light seen in escaping from a tunnel are interesting neither to those who mean to stay there nor to those who have never been there!"[24]

The second point concerns effective demand which Harrod bypassed. This remark by Keynes requires no further comment. It was fine for young critics to compare his model with the traditional one, but if they failed to see effective demand as the very essence of the *General Theory*, they would be merely bringing the latter into some nonconformable overlap with the former.

Other critical reviews of the *General Theory* appeared in 1936, with the series organized by the *Quarterly Journal of Economics* of special interest because it attracted a reply from Keynes. A substantial debate, developed in the *Economic Journal*, centered on whether it was the market for *money* or the market for *credit* that was crucial for the rate of interest. Some importance is attached to the controversy because it engendered a comparison between Keynes's theory of employment and interest and independent formulations in Sweden in the early 1930s.[25] The parallel was drawn by B. Ohlin in two articles devoted to the Stockholm School's theories of savings and investment.[26]

Ohlin noted more grounds of agreement than dispute between the Swedish approach and the *General Theory*. Yet he saw two aspects as deserving of more careful deliberation by Keynes: (1) the distinction between ex ante and ex post values of aggregate variables such as savings, investment, and income; and (2) the importance assigned to the market for money in the determination of the rate of interest.

If Keynes's savings and investment equilibrium has to reveal the underlying forces in the adjustment mechanism operative toward a stable income, Ohlin argues that these magnitudes have to be conceived in ex ante terms, that is, as *planned* values. In the

---

24. Ibid., p. 85.
25. The "Stockholm School" included the works of Gunnar Myrdal (*Der Gleichgewichtsbegriff als Instrument der Geldtheoretischen Analyse* [1933], translated under the title *Monetary Equilibrium* [London: Hodder, 1939]) and Erik Lindahl (*Penningspolitikens Medel* [1930], translated under the title *Studies in the Theory of Money and Capital* [London: G. Allen, 1939]).
26. "Some Notes on the Stockholm Theory of Saving and Investment," *The Economic Journal*, March and June 1937.

General Theory, however, they appear as ex post aggregates and thus neglect the inherent urge to equilibrium norms: instead, they merely stipulate simple accounting results. By stressing the (Stockholm view of) savings and investment plans, one must concede that generally plans and outcomes diverge, so that the discrepancy between expectations and realizations—or prospective and retrospective views—affects the next round of expectations or plans.

The obvious rebuttal is that Keynes's functional relations underlying aggregate demand clearly apply ex ante values, so this charge indicting Keynes for injecting ex post magnitudes falters. Nonetheless, an explicit distinction between ex ante and ex post values would undoubtedly have been very useful in clarifying the *General Theory* and would perhaps have avoided tedious discussions on savings and investment identity. As far as the effect of errors in forecasting in the "previous" period on *current* expectations was concerned, Ohlin, under the influence of Lindahl's important sequential analysis, was effective in questioning the meaning attached to Keynes's "equilibrium." Keynes had not pondered sufficiently the matters touched by Ohlin. The only explicit proposition that can be adduced from the *General Theory* involves entrepreneurs' reaction to "undesired" variations—as Hawtrey would conceive them—in inventories. When, in any given period, an (ex ante) excess of investment over savings drives inventories below the planned or projected level, Keynes conjectured that entrepreneurs would react with an inventory investment bulge in the subsequent period. As for discrepancies between the *expected* (ex ante) and *actual* (ex post) values of other variables, the general rule of behavior deduced from Keynes's expectations would emanate from the "convention," or the hypothesis that the present situation will prevail into the future unless there is some specific reason to expect otherwise.

With respect to the interest rate mechanism, Ohlin concurs with Keynes on the monetary nature of the phenomenon. Yet he argues that its most immediate determinants are the forces underlying the supply and demand for credit. To Ohlin the interest rate is the price that balances ex ante supply and demand for credit. He admits that credit is only one of the possible sources of investment financing and that accumulation may also be funded by using undistributed profits, liquid funds, or new share issues. In concert with Keynes, Ohlin avers that not all savings are transposed into a supply of credit; some sums can be diverted to purchase money or share capital. Nonetheless, for Ohlin "there is a connection between the dealings in claims and the activity of saving and investment" which makes it infeasible for Keynes to consider the quantity of money as the "central point" in interest rate determination.[27] It is unwarranted to claim that the interest rate depends exclusively on supply and demand for liquidity when these schedules are contingent on the supply and demand for credit which are closely linked to investment and savings decisions.

Keynes's response sensed this approach as a camouflaged return to the traditional, nonmonetary theory of the interest rate, interpreting Ohlin's concepts of the "supply and demand for credit" as the traditional supply of savings and demand for investment.[28] Yet in essence Ohlin's intervention did not entail this point, so that Keynes's resistence obscured the issue. My own view is that it is possible to partition the question into three separate aspects. For one thing, there is the dependency, in any equilibrium model, of any one condition from the rest of the conditions in the system (the so-called Walras Law). This was well clarified by Hicks in his review of the *General Theory* where he adduces that once the market for goods, and then the market for money, are in equilibrium, the same must necessarily hold for the market for bonds. If this is so it is a semantic point to contend that the interest rate is determined on the money market rather than the market for bonds.[29] In his reply to Ohlin, Keynes adverts to this argument of Hicks but fails to apply it to the immediate question.

A second quite distinct issue involves the special significance of the interest rate on money loans in a "monetary economy." As noted, there is a strategic role which the *General Theory* attaches to liquidity preference, as justified by the special characteristics of money compared to other commodities in an economy in which

---

27. Ohlin, "Alternative Theories of the Rate of Interest: Three Rejoinders," *The Economic Journal* (September 1937), p. 426.
28. "Alternative Theories of the Rate of Interest," *The Economic Journal*, June 1937.
29. Hicks, "Mr. Keynes' Theory of Employment," *The Economic Journal* (June 1963), p. 245.

wages and contracts are stipulated in money terms. From this perspective the role assigned to the demand for money is unassailable.[30]

A third vexatious matter concerns the difference between an equilibrium which involves flows and an equilibrium which deals with stocks. Ohlin does mention the sale and purchase of *pre-existing* financial assets. Nonetheless, his argument on credit, and on the link between savings and investment, compels a concentration on flow-equilibria. In practice, the scale of flows, as compared to the total stock of wealth, is rather negligible. This is why the *General Theory*'s analysis, conducted in terms of the *desired* composition of the existing stock of wealth, assumes a very weak link between flows of savings and investment and the demand for different kinds of financial assets.

An affiliated theme was touched upon in D. H. Robertson's review of the *General Theory* in which he devoted his recognized acumen to Keynes's statement that his theoretical model extracts the interest rate without recourse to the marginal efficiency of capital. Robertson declares that on Keynes's own showing of liquidity preference this cannot be true. Inasmuch as the transactions' demand for money is influenced by the profitability of investment "Mr. Keynes' theory is simply readmitting by a back door the influence on the rate of interest of that factor, namely the shape and height of the productivity curve of funds devoted to investment uses."[31]

Keynes classed this objection on a par with those of Ohlin. Nonetheless, Robertson provided a new insight: given that income and the interest rate are determined simultaneously as two endogenous variables within the model, any exogenous variation in the marginal efficiency of capital will modify both their values. Only if we consider the single behavioral function does it become impossible to fault the *General Theory* position, namely, that liquidity preference—the desire to hold a greater or a lesser proportion of a

---

30. Tobin ("A General Equilibrium Approach") dwells on the same concept, maintaining that what gives money its strategic importance in the portfolio equilibrium is the fact that, by definition, it is the only financial asset whose nominal rate of interest is constant.

31. "Some Notes on Mr. Keynes' General Theory of Employment," *The Quarterly Journal of Economics* (November 1936), p. 132.

given stock of wealth in liquid form—maintains the closest link with the interest rate.

Keynes did make some redress and defer to his critics Ohlin and Robertson. He subsequently injected the "finance motive" to include the effects of a higher level of investment as requiring "more" money, admitting that money markets could be "congested" by a lack of new cash as investment expanded.[32] The discussion on this topic is one of the unfilled sections of the *General Theory*.[33]

Special attention is merited for J. R. Hicks, particularly in view of the influence which his elaborated article has exerted on subsequent interpretations of Keynes's relationship to the classicists. Hicks's aim was "to try to construct a typical 'classical' theory, built on an earlier and cruder model than Professor Pigou,"[34] and to compare this model with the *General Theory*. Using the now commonplace symbols, Hicks summarized the classical model in equations:

$$M = kY, I = I(r), \qquad I = S(Y,r).$$

The *General Theory*, on the other hand, is collapsed into the following expressions:

$$M = L(r), I = I(r), \qquad I = S(Y).$$

The terms in a comparison of this kind resemble those of Harrod. It was natural then that Hicks concluded that liquidity preference is very important in separating Keynes from the classicists; the omission of the interest rate from Keynes's savings function is viewed as of secondary importance.

Hicks goes on to observe that a model of this type, in which the interest rate is resolved in the market for money and equilibrium follows variations in income, leads to the "singular conclusion" that an increase in the "incentive to invest" or "consume" will have

---

32. Paul Davidson has devoted his energies to this long-neglected aspect. See Davidson, *Money and the Real World* (London: Macmillan, 1972), among other writings. Earlier recognition appears in Weintraub, *An Approach to the Theory of Income Distribution*.

33. Cf. also Weintraub, "Hicksian Keynesianism: Dominance and Decline," in *Modern Economic Thought*, ed. Weintraub (Philadelphia: University of Pennsylvania Press, 1977).

34. Hicks, "Mr. Keynes and the Classicists," p. 148.

repercussions on income, leaving the interest rate unvaried. This however, he immediately observes, is not the *General Theory* but rather Keynes's *special* theory, since the only component in the demand for money is the speculative motive, whereas Keynes himself had introduced other income-linked motives as well. A more accurate model of the *General Theory* would thus entail:

$$M = L(Y,r), \qquad I = I(r), \qquad I = S(Y,r).$$

Hicks's judgment is that in this "Mr. Keynes takes a big step back to Marshallian orthodoxy, and his theory becomes hard to distinguish from the revised and qualified Marshallian theories."[35]

What then distinguishes Keynes from the classical economists? To assess the novelty Hicks constructs the curve for establishing equilibrium between the supply and demand for money (*LL*) and the supply and demand for investment (*IS*), both in the (r,Y) plane. Hicks then shows that when the marginal efficiency of capital increases, it is the initial position of the *IS* curve which determines whether the outcome will be standard classical theory or the *General Theory*. If *IS* initially cuts *LL* where the latter is horizontal, a rightward shift implies more income at an unchanged r. On the other hand, if *IS* cuts the tail section of *LL* the result is a higher r with flat income. Over intermediate points a rightward dislodgement of *IS* lifts both Y and r, but the extra Y is tapered compared to that obtainable with a constant r.

Interpreting this as the essence of the *General Theory*, it is pure fantasy to think that Keynes's message could ever have been the basis for a theoretical revolution, or that it could have stimulated economists to ferret out new analytical theses for the study of the laws underlying capitalism. Presented in the Hicksian way, the *General Theory*, with its wealth of real-world perplexities, was subverted to a plain, arid, equation model whose main novelty lay in the "liquidity trap." Surely, the *General Theory*, with its central focus on money in the stability of capitalism's accumulation mechanism, probed far more delicate troubles. Doubtless, Modigliani and Klein enriched our analytic insight into Keynes. But they, too, were under Hicks's original spell.[36]

---

35. Ibid., p. 153.

36. Modigliani, "Liquidity Preference," and "The Money Mechanism"; and L. Klein, "Theories of Effective Demand and Employment," *The Journal of Political Economy*, April 1947, and *The Keynesian Revolution* (New York: Macmillan, 1949).

My own view is that the understanding of the role of effective demand in accumulation has been obscured in the models of the so-called neoclassical synthesis. Concealed within is the incompatibility between effective demand and the neoclassical general equilibrium theory, diverting attention from the essence of Keynes's equilibrium. James Tobin has detected the complexities engendered when the theory of the portfolio equilibrium is extended to the equities market involving the market's evaluation of the existing capital goods stock, considered in concert with entrepreneurs' expectations of rates of return on new capital goods.[37] Tobin's solution espouses a recognition of two different rates of return, and thus of different prices for old and new capital goods living side by side.

The coherence of this "solution" with the *General Theory* is dubious. Observed above (chapter 8) was that the prices of existing capital goods will adjust rapidly to changing expectations, and that entrepreneurs switch their investment demand from new to old goods and vice versa, thereby balancing their respective prices.[38]

Tobin's method is hardly a unique way of escaping one of the traditional equilibrium conditions in order to make room for effective demand. An alternative, for instance, would have been to stress the under-utilization of all factors, and not just of labor, embracing a conception which could extend the main propositions of the *General Theory* to the long term. Certainly Keynes could more convincingly espouse a long-run vista of stable underemployment than a configuration marked by a prolonged imbalance in different rates of return.[39]

Don Patinkin's attempt to present the *General Theory* as a special case of orthodox theory confirms the damages along the Hicksian road which disparaged the gulf separating Keynes from classicism.[40] It is fascinating to find that Patinkin deduces all the

---

37. See his "Money, Capital and Other Stores of Values," and "A General Equilibrium Approach."

38. For the process visualized as balancing the "demand" price for existing capital goods with their marginal cost of production, and thus with the "supply price" for new investment, see Keynes, "The Theory of the Rate of Interest in the Lessons of Monetary Experience" (1937); reprinted in *C.W.K.* 14:102.

39. For my own analysis in this direction see my "Disoccupazione e prezzi relativi: Un tentativo di reinterpretazione di Keynes," in *La controversia Keynesiana*.

40. *Money, Interest and Prices* (New York: Harper and Row, 1965).

significant implications of the Hicks-Modigliani-Klein interpretative paradigm, underwriting a Keynesian model differing only from past orthodoxy by a number of rigidities and specific hypotheses. Unemployment dissipates into a transitory phenomenon which manifests itself through entrepreneurial reactions to excessive inventory accumulation. Patinkin's entrepreneurs, facing a reduction in aggregate demand, produce and accumulate inventories up to some certain critical point, and thereafter cut their demand for labor. Under a "downward rigidity" of money wages, real wages are steady so that employment diverges from the optimal level; in other words, business firms hire less labor than is specified at the real wage on the demand curve for labor.

Firms are thus slow to extricate themselves from the disequilibrium. "Involuntary" unemployment is in flower until, over time, through appropriate variations in prices and wages, the system is restored toward full employment with only "voluntary" unemployment predominating.[41]

---

41. This sketch of "involuntary" unemployment as a dynamic disequilibrium phenomenon is confirmed in Patinkin's later work ("Keynes' Monetary Thought: A Study of Its Development," *History of Political Economy*, Spring 1976).

CHAPTER 11

THE SIGNIFICANCE
OF KEYNES'S EQUILIBRIUM

The criticisms contained in most reviews of the *General Theory* tended to seize on specific points. Few devoted themselves to its more general significance as a theoretical vision, as a political economy of capitalism. Even today, nearly half a century after the *General Theory* appeared, this aspect is still open. Of the many facets of the debate on the significance of Keynes's work not unconnected to the stagflation crisis from which the Western world has been suffering since the early 1970s, I propose to confine myself here to a number of striking ideas which impose themselves from a complete reading (or rereading) of Keynes's works.[1]

A first observation is that Keynes cannot be reduced to the *General Theory*. Too many evaluations of Keynes dwell exclusively on this one book.[2] This is certainly true when Keynes is charged with having ignored the menace of inflation, or of reasoning in terms of aggregate demand and ignoring changes in its composition, or of dwelling only on fluctuations in income rather than on its growth over time. The *General Theory* was neither the starting point nor

---

1. On the stagflation crisis, with acknowledged intellectual debts to Keynes, the work of Sidney Weintraub has been particularly conspicuous. See, as one example, his *Capitalism, Inflation, and Unemployment Crisis*.

2. Even Marxist interpretations of Keynes have ended up by following the traditional interpretative approach, concentrating on certain specific propositions contained in the *General Theory* and neglecting themes, which they would have undoubtedly found more congenial, in Keynes's earlier writings. See for example Klein, "Theories of Effective Demand"; P. Mattick, *Marx and Keynes: The Limits of the Mixed Economy* (London: Merlin Press, 1969); and the essays in D. Horowitz, *Marx and Modern Economics* (London: MacGibbon and Kee, 1968).

the terminus for Keynes's reflections on capitalism, though it was the culmination of his theoretical work as an economist.

A brief enumeration of his analyses testifies to the range of his conjectures. There were the role of financial institutions as one of the "historically given" mechanisms underlying monetary economies; the bases of the capitalist accumulation process and the cause of their instability; the limits to the validity of the "rules of the game" and "laissez-faire" stabilization policies for controlling crises; the endogenous causes of variations in the value of money.

These are a brief catalogue of the stages in Keynes's research into the facts that sum up the logic of the capitalist system. When the economic crisis of the 1930s alerted Keynes to the need to abandon the last safe anchorage point—the assumption of constant real income—in the theoretical credo he had inherited from his masters, he was inspired, this time in a global perspective, to seek out the basic laws of capitalism. Is it possible to express concretely, in a series of propositions, how capitalism works? This was Keynes's query immediately after the *Treatise on Money*. His reflections had to ponder whether the behavior of the economic actors, the way institutions functioned, and the influence of metaeconomic phenomena, could be epitomized by rules of conduct sufficiently stable and generalized to be stylized in analytical (not necessarily algebraic) propositions.

The *General Theory* presumes that it is possible to identify the rules of conduct deduced, not, as in Walras's general equilibrium, on the basis of an illusory maximizing rationality, but rather from observed fact. Also, what is needed to compose these rules into a system for interpreting reality is not the stability of the behavioral functions themselves but rather the understanding of the economic logic urging them to change. Once it is ascertained, for example, that the marginal efficiency of capital is a highly unstable function, what really counts is to apply economic reasoning to explain its directional shifts.

Hicks decided that the "method of expectations," as used by Keynes, is "the most revolutionary thing in this book."[3] Yet he tended to set Keynes into the box occupied by the Swedish school with its ex ante and ex post comparisons and in which the degree of realism of the theory depends substantially on the length of the time period

---

3. "Mr. Keynes' Theory of Employment," p. 240.

for which expectations are assumed to hold. This merging of Keynes's "method of expectations" with the Swedish period equilibrium method, which Hicks himself adopts in *Value and Capital*, is arbitrary. J. A. Kregel has since emphasized that Keynes's thinking on expectations came more naturally from a consolidated Cambridge tradition which had little in common with the Swedish approach.[4] Kregel rightly argues that Keynes's method is based not on "constant" expectations over an arbitrary time interval but rather on *given expectations at one point in time*. This also explains Keynes's insistence, after the *General Theory* had been published, that the possibility of unemployment equilibrium is independent of any discrepancy between ex ante and ex post values.

The innovation in the *General Theory*'s "method of expectations" as compared to traditional theory is that the systemic data now include not only techniques of production, preferences, and initial resources, but also people's expectations for the future. This makes it possible to determine the values that prices and quantities may assume as expectations vary. The methodological limitations of Keynes's "shifting equilibrium" adhere to the fact that each period is considered in a sense as in isolation, making it impossible as a rule to establish a unique set of long-term prices and quantities to which the system tends.[5]

It follows that an evaluation of Keynes's equilibrium method depends on a judgment concerning the forces tending to move the system toward specific long-term values. Classical economists (in Marx's categorization) devoted themselves, for example, to determining a uniform rate of profit evolving from a set of "normal" prices, explained by their theory of value. Conversely, current prices could reflect mere accidental shifts away from the deeper reality; the temporary deviations were supposed to be corrected by competition. Taking real wages as fixed (exogenously) at subsistence levels, and with production determined independently of values, classical

---

4. J. A. Kregel, "Economic Methodology in the Face of Uncertainty," *The Economic Journal*, June 1976, and "On the Existence of Expectations in English Neoclassical Economies," *Journal of Economic Literature*, June 1977.

5. An interesting analysis of the possibility that mobile equilibrium situations might converge toward long-term equilibrium positions is presented by Sergio Parrinello in "Note sulla nozione di equilibrio in economia politica," *Giornale degli Economisti*, January–February 1977.

theory could then describe "normal prices" as "centers of gravitation" toward which current prices had to converge in the long run.[6]

These "centers of gravitation" were anchored in the classical theory of savings and investment. Except for Thomas R. Malthus, the classicists held investment as identically equal to savings (Say's Law), with the key variable regulating accumulation being the rate of profit. As capital accumulates, the profit rate falls. This was the only link between quantities and values, and its force was such as to forestall any doubts over the effective existence of centers of gravitation: the impulses transmitted from quantities to prices via the rate of profit were very regular and slow to act. On this kind of interpretation of capitalism, a short-run analysis, based exclusively on the formation of current prices, suffered the limitations denounced by Marx as "vulgar" economics.

Is Keynes's theory subject to similar limitations? Does the *General Theory* model contain "centers of gravitation"? We have noted that Keynes rejected the "classical" (in his sense of classical) "natural" interest rate equating the supply of savings and the demand for investment. Granting his assault to be unsatisfactory, he is very adamant that the interest rate is a "conventional," money phenomenon, tied to particular historical-institutional facts within the system. It is thus the marginal efficiency of capital which is activated by the money rate of interest, driving the scale of investment according to expectations and the supply price for new capital goods. Expectations, however, are volatile, so that as a result instability permeates the entire investment process. Here, in his telling, Keynes has wandered far from Wicksell's position of a stable rate of profit toward which long-term money interest rates converge. This is not all. The instability of investment is transmitted, and amplified, in real income and employment, and finally in the price level and real wages. Where then are the long-term gravitational prices?

If long-term values are precluded one cannot fault an analysis that prevents convergence to them! If it is believed that the theoretical analysis of the working of an economic system requires centers of gravitation (or long-term equilibrium positions) as fundamental

---

6. This term, introduced by Adam Smith, is used by P. Garegnani in "On a Change in the Notion of Equilibrium in Recent Work on Value: A Comment on Samuelson," in *Essays in Modern Capital Theory*, ed. M. Brown, K. Sato, and P. Zarembka (North Holland, 1976).

reference points to which current magnitudes tend after being released from exogenous factors and imperfections of every kind, then the critique of Keynes has to shift ground from the method to the theory itself.

On this view, can one accept Keynes's theory of the capitalist system? In particular, one has to ponder why long-term positions are omitted from the *General Theory*. By his rejection of Say's Law, Keynes had to confront the traditional theory of interest and replace the idea of a full employment interest rate with that of a money rate connected to institutional factors.[7] Undoubtedly, on its hypotheses, the full employment rate constitutes, for the traditional theory, a theoretically valid gravitational center,[8] and in abandoning it Keynes discarded any chance at a long-run analysis. But the very rejection of the position that investment automatically adjusts to full employment savings generates Keynes's model built on the variability of income, and providing a general theory of employment.

Keynes simply had to abandon Say's Law, for its incongruity is implicit in his whole vision of capitalism's failures. An economic system in which private capital accumulation is regulated exclusively by decisions to save is an abstract system, although during a specific phase of the history of capitalism, when savers and investors were to a large extent one and the same people, Say's Law may have been pertinent. For Keynes and the system he observed for so long, decisions to invest are vital for growth. Moreover, there is absolutely no mechanism to guarantee that investment will stabilize at some long-term norm, or that its variation over time adheres to a regular law. Uncertainty, expectations, and the fragility of the "convention" are not mere imperfections or frictions but structural phenomena in capitalism. They are the essence of capitalism.

The economic relevance of the notion of equilibrium has recently been questioned by N. Kaldor,[9] who renounces the high abstraction and unrealism implicit in the concept of general economic

---

7. For a brilliant assessment of Keynes's theory of interest, see G. L. S. Shackle, *The Years of High Theory* (Cambridge: At the University Press, 1967), chap. 15.

8. As we have already seen, theoretical validity is limited to Walras's interpretation of the traditional theory.

9. "The Irrelevance of Equilibrium Economics," *The Economic Journal*, December 1972.

equilibrium, either in Walras's original version or in more recent work set out most completely by G. Debreu.[10] Kaldor invokes the specter of increasing returns to scale, a phenomenon incompatible with Walras's equilibrium model. He traces "increasing returns" as originating in Adam Smith's principle of the division of labor, and reviews Allyn Young's important analysis of the interaction between innovation, increasing returns, and economic growth.[11] This analysis emphasizes the endogenous stimulus to growth of an initial broadening of markets which can make better use of resources in a "virtuous circle of growth."

Under increasing returns the notion of equilibrium, in Walras's or Pareto's sense of efficient resource allocation, disintegrates. Does this deprive equilibrium of its meaning? In response to Kaldor's attack, F. H. Hahn has recently proposed a definition of equilibrium that transcends Walras's conception. According to Hahn "an economy is in equilibrium when it generates messages which do not cause agents to change the theories which they hold or the policies which they pursue."[12]

It is not easy to decide whether this notion of equilibrium actually answers the criticisms raised. The real problem is whether the concept of equilibrium is a useful homing point in studying reality, which in practice resembles a magma in continual flux. This impels a definition of equilibrium with hypotheses which do not contradict the reality we are trying to understand. A negative example lies in growth models in which the equilibrium condition entails that all variables grow steadily at the same rate over time. Capitalist development, however, is a story of erratic capital growth; steady growth is an anomaly and any such notion of "equilibrium" is completely irrelevant. On the "steady growth" method of analysis, the system is only in equilibrium when it is not behaving "normally."

On several occasions Keynes defines his *General Theory* as a short-term analysis in Marshall's sense that productive capacity is

10. "Theory of Value: An Axiomatic Analysis of Economic Equilibrium," *Cowles Foundation Monograph*, no. 17 (New York, 1959).

11. A. Young, "Increasing Returns and Economic Progress," *The Economic Journal*, December 1928.

12. *On the Notion of Equilibrium in Economics* (Cambridge: At the University Press, 1973), p. 25.

given, while his method entailing a "theory of shifting equilibrium" implies "the theory of a system in which changing views about the future are capable of influencing the present situation."

This is a fundamental consequence of the presence of money, whose importance "essentially flows from its being a link between the present and the future."[13] For Keynes the possibility that the relation between money, employment, and prices that governs the scene in this short-term equilibrium may converge in the long run toward "simpler" propositions is "a question for historical generalization rather than for pure theory." He remarks that "the very long-run course of prices has almost always been upward. For when money is relatively abundant, the wage-unit rises; and when money is relatively scarce, some means is found to increase the effective quantity of money."[14] The average level of long-run employment depends on the historical conditions influencing the marginal efficiency of capital, and on the minimum rate of interest which wealth-owners require in accepting nonliquid financial assets:

> During the nineteenth century, the growth of population and of invention, the opening-up of new lands, the state of confidence and the frequency of war over the average of (say) each decade seem to have been sufficient, taken in conjunction with the propensity to consume, to establish a schedule of the marginal efficiency of capital which allowed a reasonably satisfactory average level of employment to be compatible with a rate of interest high enough to be psychologically acceptable to wealth-owners.[15]

In a historical situation less favorable to capital accumulation, and in socioinstitutional conditions that encourage liquidity preference, employment may not get so close to full employment, and increases in the money quantity may prove to be an ineffective unemployment remedy. In treating the long period in this way, Keynes may appear to be avoiding the problem.

Pierangelo Garegnani has recently argued that Keynes's analysis supports recent neoclassical efforts to abort the long-period analysis in favor of short-period equilibrium.[16] According to Ga-

13. Keynes, *General Theory*, in *C.W.K.* 7:293.
14. Ibid., p. 307.
15. Ibid.
16. "On a Change in the Notion of Equilibrium."

regnani, this affirmation takes both a direct and an implicit turn. Indirectly, it appears in Hicks's critique of "natural" prices founded on their omission of expectations;[17] more directly it derives from the *General Theory's* move from partial equilibrium analysis, where capital theory had been confined, to an analysis of the whole equilibrium system.

Hicks rationalizes his rejection of the long period, in which a uniform rate of returns emerges on all capital goods, on the need to distinguish between *current* and *expected* prices. Garegnani holds that the real reason for this rejection is the implicit contradictions in the neoclassical theory of capital, making it logically impossible to conceive of demand for capital as a single-value magnitude related to the rate of profit via the law of marginal productivity. Therefore, Keynes's expectational method is not apprehended as a valid justification for a rejection of the classical methodology.

In practice, Garegnani holds that Keynes's main intent was to erect an adjustment mechanism between savings and investment where income was a variable, and that his aim in introducing expectations and liquidity preference was "to provide an alternative to the orthodox doctrine of interest as the equilibrator of saving and investment."[18]

As the traditional theory of interest erected a barrier for Keynes to overcome, the "expectations" method "through liquidity preference and the instability of marginal efficiency of capital . . . had the main role of providing him with a provisional way out of the conflict between his initial novelty and the dominant theory of distribution."[19] Keynes's mechanism to insure that savings adjust to investment via income variations becomes clothed as a proposition which "was, in itself, independent of the method of expectations and was not necessarily confined to the short period."[20] Garegnani concludes that "the *General Theory* does not seem to offer real ground for the contemporary attempt to rework traditional theory in terms of short-period equilibria."[21]

By-passing the substance of this last statement of Garegnani,

17. *Value and Capital*, 2d ed. (New York: Oxford University Press, 1946).

18. "On a Change in the Notion of Equilibrium," p. 41.

19. Ibid., pp. 40, 41.

20. Ibid., p. 40.

21. Ibid., p. 42.

it is possible to argue that he tends to understate the place of expectations in Keynes, viewing liquidity preference and the instability of the marginal efficiency of capital as mere means to the multiplier end. Sentences extracted by Garegnani from Keynes's reply to Ohlin and Hawtrey scarcely sustain his verdict.[22]

---

22. A sentence quoted by Garegnani reads as follows: "As I have said above, the initial novelty lies in my maintaining that it is not the rate of interest, but the level of incomes which ensures equality between saving and investment. The arguments that lead up to this initial conclusion are independent of my subsequent theory of the rate of interest, and in fact I reached it before I had reached the latter theory. But the result of it was to leave the rate of interest in the air" (Keynes, "Alternative Theories of the Rate of Interest," p. 250).

To understand the full sense of the passage we should consider the context to which it belongs. Keynes's aim was to reply to Hawtrey, who had claimed that in the *General Theory* savings and investment are *identically* equal. The point he insisted on was that savings and investment are equal but that, as in the case of the supply and demand for any good, this equality is *not* the same thing as an identity, and finally that this equality is obtained through variations in income, and not in the interest rate. The sentence to which Keynes referred ("As I have said"), at the beginning of the passage quoted by Garegnani, reads: "It was never suggested that saving and investment could be unequal. This idea arose (for the first time, so far as I am aware) with certain post-war theories. In maintaining the equality of saving and investment, I am, therefore, returning to old-fashioned orthodoxy. The novelty in my treatment of saving and investment consists, not in my maintaining their necessary aggregate equality, but in the proposition that it is, not the rate of interest, but the level of income which (in conjunction with certain other factors) ensure this equality" (Ibid., pp. 248–49).

In reality this specification does not explain the order in which Keynes formulated the various sections of his theory. I would argue, however, that the actual stages in the development of his thinking (on which this book is based) are a more solid point of reference than his own ex-post reconstruction for polemical ends. Garegnani quotes another sentence: "To speak of the 'Liquidity-preference Theory' of the Rate of interest is, indeed, to dignify it too much." Here too, however, the context is polemical, as is shown by the sentence which follows (and which Garegnani omits): "It is like speaking of the 'Professorship Theory' of Ohlin or the 'Civil-Servant Theory' of Hawtrey" (Ibid., p. 252). At the same time, however, one has to grant Garegnani that it is hard to exaggerate the importance of Keynes's statement, to be found a little further on: "I am simply stating what it is, the significant theories on the subject being subsequent."

The question that Keynes has posed immediately following the publication of the *Treatise*, and which he grappled with logically, was the classical theory of interest as he detected effective demand to be the crucial innovation indissolubly tied to the instability characteristic of a monetary economy, with appendages in bouts of liquidity preference and the instability tremors in the marginal efficiency of capital.[23] These categories contained the images of Keynes's vision of capitalism. Inevitably his theory must clash with the traditional theory, not in analytical thinking about capital alone, but rather over the autonomy of the decisions to accumulate. Even the most rigorous recital of the traditional theory by Walras has its genesis in Say's Law, a vision of capitalism dramatically at odds with that of Keynes.

If, as I have argued, the *General Theory* is nothing more than the culmination of Keynes's vision of capitalism, it follows that the significance of Keynes's equilibrium conception impels a judgment on his whole accomplishment as an economist. It was a grinding march on a long path from his *Indian Currency and Finance* to the *General Theory* as he gradually shaped his theoretical edifice.

Keynes is not merely an economist who introduced effective demand, or liquidity preference, into the neoclassical substructures; those who construe him in these limited equational terms or consider him as a mere modifier of the traditional orthodoxy, have done Keynes a disservice. It is hard to deny the relevance for the profession of the Hicks-Modigliani-Klein interpretative paradigm, or of the analyses by Patinkin and by Robert Clower and Axel Leijonhufvud.[24] Yet, in this paradigm Keynes's contribution to the analysis of capitalism appears sterile. There has been a systematic elimination of any strand in Keynes's thinking that cannot be rendered in a stylized model of the economic system, squeezed of any socioinstitutional reference or complexities, or of the intrinsic instability of the capitalist accumulation process.

---

23. Cf. Keynes's draft of "The Parameters of a Monetary Economy" (chap. 7 above).

24. R. W. Clower, "The Keynesian Counter-Revolution: A Theoretical Appraisal," in *The Theory of Interest Rates*, ed. F. H. Hahn and F. Brechling (London: Macmillan, 1965); and A. Leijonhufvud, *On Keynesian Economics and the Economics of Keynes* (New York: Oxford University Press, 1968).

In his later works Keynes takes the historical and institutional relevance of financial structures, which had been at the center of the debate in *Indian Currency and Finance*, as known. Subsequent interpretative literature has curiously reduced the whole matter to a reference to the "money supply." The devastating inflation with its effects on private capital accumulation, and on income distribution, which are so vital a part of his *Economic Consequences of the Peace*, has been ignored so completely that Keynes has even been accused of having neglected inflation! His reflections on the advent of a new era in capitalism in which the trade unions assume a commanding political and economic role, expressed so clearly in "Am I a Liberal?," has left virtually no mark on Keynesians.

The instability, and fragility, of decisions to invest, in a world in which money payments involve a time interval between expenditure and receipts, have been rendered as a stable relation between investment and the interest rate. Some have even gone so far as to identify the marginal efficiency of capital with the "marginal productivity" of capital. Crises, and the endogenous mechanisms which feed them—the central theme in the *Treatise on Money*—have been almost completely forgotten. Keynes's structural analyses criticizing the Bradbury Commission, and its suggestions for resolving the Lancashire cotton crisis, have never won due recognition: Keynes has been shrunken to an economist identified with aggregate analysis.

At the theoretical level, instead of developing problems left open by the *General Theory*, Keynesian literature has crystallized themes to which Keynes carefully avoided simplistic responses in terms of "analytically convenient" solutions. Problems raised by Keynes have often been relegated to the shadows of the short period, while other Keynesians have gone on to the theory of economic growth by adapting investment to an exogenously determined income growth. The contradiction is astonishing. Other significant examples include the neglect, for a long time, of the Stock Exchange in portfolio theory and in decisions to accumulate, and failures to ponder the redistributive effects of inflation.[25]

For economic policy the paradoxical result has been that from

---

25. For significant exceptions to the rule see Tobin, Davidson, *Money and the Real World*; and H. P. Minsky, *John Maynard Keynes* (New York: Columbia University Press, 1975).

the mid 1940s to the mid 1960s, when there existed a series of factors favorable to stable capital formation, Keynesian analysis was seen as a valid means of controlling aggregate demand and its various components. Recalling capitalism's predisposition to recurrent crises, this period was atypical. This implies that the economic reality which Keynes studied was devoid of crises of distribution and accumulation, and reduced to a world in which a friction-free supply adapted instantaneously to moves in relative prices, so that the only important role was played by demand.[26] This can also explain why subsequent instability has engendered skepticism over Keynesian analysis.

The whole body of Keynes's works is based on precisely the opposite premises! The stimulus to his analysis was always some moment of capitalist crisis. The absurd reduction of his thinking to a succinct list of fiscal and monetary maneuvers is a direct consequence of the reductive interpretations of his work which mark—and mar—the literature. Keynes's thought has direct relevance to the present moment of capitalist crisis. We might well heed the warning that Keynes uttered more than half a century ago:

> We have changed, by insensible degrees, our philosophy of economic life, our notions of what is reasonable and what is tolerable; and we have done this without changing our technique or our copybook maxims. Hence our tears and troubles.[27]

---

26. For a critique of this traditional interpretation of Keynes see J. Robinson, "The Second Crisis of Economic Theory," *The American Economic Review*, Papers and Proceedings, 1972.

27. Keynes, "Am I a Liberal?," in *C.W.K.* 9:306.

WORKS CITED

Ando, A., and Modigliani, F. "The Life Cycle Hypothesis of Savings: Aggregate Implications and Tests." *American Economic Review*, March 1963.

Becattini, G. "Introduzione." In *Economia della Produzione*. Italian edition of *Economics of Production*, by A. Marshall and M. P. Marshall (1879). Milan: ISEDI, 1975.

Böhm-Bawerk, E. von. *Positive Theory of Capital*. London: Macmillan, 1891.

Caffè, F. "Keynes e i suoi contemporanei." *Note Economiche*, September–December 1975.

Chandler, L. V. *Benjamin Strong Central Banker*. Washington, D.C.: The Brookings Institution, 1958.

Ciocca, P. "L'ipotesi del ritardo dei salari rispetto ai prezzi in periodi di inflazione: Alcune considerazioni generali." *Bancaria*, May 1969.

Clower, R. W. "The Keynesian Counter-Revolution: A Theoretical Appraisal." In *The Theory of Interest Rates*, edited by F. H. Hahn and F. Brechling. London: Macmillan, 1965.

Davidson, P. *Money and the Real World*. London: Macmillan, 1972.

———. "The Dual-Faceted Nature of the Keynesian Revolution: Money and Money Wages in Unemployment and Production Flow Prices." *Journal of Post-Keynesian Economics*, Fall 1980.

Debreu, G. "Theory of Value: An Axiomatic Analysis of Economic Equilibrium." *Cowles Foundation Monograph*, no. 17. New York, 1959.

De Vecchi, N. *Valore e profitto nell'economia politica classica*. Milan: Feltrinelli, 1976.

Fisher, I. *The Purchasing Power of Money*. New York: Macmillan, 1911.

———. *The Theory of Interest*. 1930. Reprint. New York: Kelley and Millan, 1954.

———. "The Debt-Deflation Theory of Great Depressions." *Econometrica* (1933), pp. 337–57.

Fleisig, V. H. "War-related Debts and the Great Depression." *American Economic Review*. Papers and Proceedings, May 1976.

Garegnani, P. *Il capitale nelle teorie della distribuzione*. Milan: Giuffrè, 1960.

―――. "Heterogeneous Capital, the Production Function and the Theory of Distribution." *The Review of Economic Studies*, July 1970.

―――. "On a Change in the Notion of Equilibrium in Recent Work on Value: A Comment on Samuelson." In *Essays in Modern Capital Theory*, edited by M. Brown, K. Sato, and P. Zarembka. North Holland, 1976.

Hahn, F. H. *On the Notion of Equilibrium in Economics: An Inaugural Lecture*. Cambridge: At the University Press, 1973.

Harcourt, G. C. *Some Cambridge Controversies in the Theory of Capital*. Cambridge: At the University Press, 1972.

Harrod, R. F. "Mr. Keynes and the Traditional Theory." *Econometrica*, January 1937.

―――. *The Life of John Maynard Keynes*. London: Macmillan, 1951.

Hawtrey, R. G. *Monetary Reconstruction*. London: Longmans, 1926.

―――. *Capital and Employment*. London: Longmans, 1936.

Hayek, F. A. von. *Prices and Production*. London: G. Routledge and Sons, 1931.

―――. "Reflections on the Pure Theory of Money of Mr. J. M. Keynes." *Economica*, August 1931.

―――. "The Pure Theory of Money: A Rejoinder." *Economica*, November 1931.

―――. "Money and Capital: A Reply." *The Economic Journal*, June 1932.

Hicks, J. R. "Mr. Keynes' Theory of Employment." *The Economic Journal*, June 1936.

―――. "Mr. Keynes and the 'Classics': A Suggested Interpretation." *Econometrica*, January 1937.

―――. *Value and Capital*. 2d ed. New York: Oxford University Press, 1946.

―――. *Crisis in Keynesian Economics*. Oxford: Blackwell, 1974.

Horowitz, D. *Marx and Modern Economics*. London: MacGibbon and Kee, 1968.

Hume, D. *On the Balance of Trade*. 1752. Reprinted in D. Hume, *Writings on Economics*, edited by E. Rotwein. Edinburgh: Nelson, 1955.

Kaldor, N. "The Irrelevance of Equilibrium Economics." *The Economic Journal*, December 1972.

Keynes, J. M. *Indian Currency and Finance*. London: Macmillan, 1913. Reprinted in *C.W.K.*, vol. 1.

―――. *Memorandum on Proposals for the Establishment of a State Bank in India*. 1913. Reprinted in *C.W.K.* 15:151–214.

―――. "War and the Financial System." *The Economic Journal*, August 1914.

―――. *The Economic Consequences of the Peace*. London: Macmillan, 1919. Reprinted in *C.W.K.*, vol. 2.

―――. *A Treatise on Probability*. London: Macmillan, 1921. Reprinted in *C.W.K.*, vol. 8.

―――. *A Revision of the Treaty*. London: Macmillan, 1922. Reprinted in *C.W.K.*, vol. 3.

―――. Reconstruction Supplements of the *Manchester Guardian Commercial*. "The Theory of the Exchanges and Purchasing Power Parity," 20 April 1922; "The Forward Market in Foreign Exchange," 20 April 1922; "Inflation as a Method of Taxation," 27 July 1922; "The Consequences to Society of Changes in the Value of Money," 27 July 1922.

―――. *A Tract on Monetary Reform*. London: Macmillan, 1923. Reprinted in *C.W.K.*, vol. 4.

―――. "Alfred Marshall 1842–1924." *The Economic Journal*, September 1924. Reprinted in *C.W.K.*, vol. 10.

―――. "The Committee on the Currency." Notes and Memoranda. *The Economic Journal*, June 1925.

―――. *The Economic Consequences of Mr. Churchill*. London: Hogarth Press, 1925. Reprinted in *C.W.K.*, vol. 9.

―――. "Am I a Liberal?" *Nation and Athenaeum*, 8 and 15 August 1925. Reprinted in *C.W.K.*, vol. 9.

―――. *A Short View of Russia*. 1925. Reprinted in *C.W.K.*, vol. 9.

―――. *The End of Laissez-faire*. London: Hogarth Press, 1926. Reprinted in *C.W.K.*, vol. 9.

―――, in collaboration with H. Henderson. "Can Lloyd George Do It?" Partially published in *Nation and Athenaeum*, 11 May 1929. Reprinted in *C.W.K.*, vol. 9.

―――. *Economic Possibilities for Our Grand Children*. 1930. Reprinted in *C.W.K.*, vol. 9.

―――. "F. P. Ramsey as an Economist." *The Economic Journal*, 1930. Reprinted in *C.W.K.*, vol. 10.

―――. *A Treatise on Money*. 2 vols. London: Macmillan, 1930. Reprinted in *C.W.K.*, vols. 5 and 6.

―――. *An Economic Analysis of Unemployment*. 1931. Reprinted in *C.W.K.*, vol. 13.

―――. "Rejoinder." *The Economic Journal*, September 1931.

―――. "Ramsey as Philosopher." *The New Statesman and Nation*, 3 October 1931. Reprinted in *C.W.K.*, vol. 10.

―――. "The Pure Theory of Money: A Reply to Dr. Hayek." *Economica*, November 1931.

―――. "A Monetary Theory of Production." *Festschrift für Arthur Spiethoff*. 1933. Reprinted in *C.W.K.*, vol. 13.

————. *The General Theory of Employment, Interest and Money.* London: Macmillan, 1936. Reprinted in *C.W.K.*, vol. 7.

————. "William Stanley Jevons." *Journal of the Royal Statistical Society.* 1936. Reprinted in *C.W.K.*, vol. 10.

————. "The General Theory of Employment." *The Quarterly Journal of Economics*, February 1937.

————. "The Theory of the Rate of Interest in the Lessons of Monetary Experience: Essays in Honour of Irving Fisher." 1937. Reprinted in *C.W.K.*, vol. 14.

————. "Alternative Theories of the Rate of Interest." *The Economic Journal*, June 1937.

————. *Dr. Melchior: A Defeated Enemy.* Published posthumously under the title *Two Memoirs*, edited by Rupert Hart-Davis. Reprinted in *C.W.K.* 10:389–429.

Klein, L. "Theories of Effective Demand and Employment." *The Journal of Political Economy*, April 1947.

————. *The Keynesian Revolution.* New York: Macmillan, 1949.

Kregel, J. A. "Economic Methodology in the Face of Uncertainty." *The Economic Journal*, June 1976.

————. "On the Existence of Expectations in English Neoclassical Economies." *Journal of Economic Literature*, June 1977.

Leijonhufvud, A. *On Keynesian Economics and the Economics of Keynes: A Study in Monetary Theory.* New York: Oxford University Press, 1968.

Lindahl, E. *Penningspolitikens Medel.* 1930. Translated under the title *Studies in the Theory of Money and Capital.* London: G. Allen, 1939.

Lunghini, G. *La crisi dell'economia politica e la teoria del valore.* Milan: Feltrinelli, 1977.

Malthus, R. *Principles of Political Economy.* 1820. Reprint. Oxford: Basil Blackwell, A. M. Kelly, 1951.

Marshall, A. *Principles of Economics.* 8th ed. London: Macmillan, 1920.

————. *Money, Credit and Commerce.* London: Macmillan, 1923.

Mattick, P. *Marx and Keynes: The Limits of the Mixed Economy.* London: Merlin Press, 1969.

Minsky, H. P. *John Maynard Keynes.* New York: Columbia University Press, 1975.

————. "An Economics of Keynes' Perspective on Money." In *Modern Economic Thought*, edited by S. Weintraub. Philadelphia: University of Pennsylvania Press, 1977.

Modigliani, F. "Liquidity Preference and the Theory of Interest and Money." *Econometrica* (1944), pp. 45–88.

————. "The Monetary Mechanism and Its Interreaction with Real Phenomena." *The Review of Economics and Statistics*, February 1963.

Moggridge, D. E. *British Monetary Policy, 1924–31.* Cambridge: At the University Press, 1972.

———, ed. *Keynes—Aspects of the Man and His Work.* London: Macmillan, 1974.

Morishima, M. "Leon Walras and Money." In *Current Economic Problems*, edited by M. Makin and A. R. Nobay. Cambridge: At the University Press, 1975.

———. *Walras' Economics.* Cambridge: At the University Press, 1977.

Myrdal, G. *Der Gleichgewichtsbegriff als Instrument der Geldtheoretischen Analyse.* 1933. Translated under the title *Monetary Equilibrium.* London: Hodye, 1939.

Ohlin, B. "Some Notes on the Stockholm Theory of Saving and Investment." *The Economic Journal*, March and June 1937.

———. "Alternative Theories of the Rate of Interest: Three Rejoinders." *The Economic Journal*, September 1937.

Parrinello, S. "Note sulla nozione di equilibrio in economia politica." *Giornale degli Economisti*, January–February 1977.

Pasinetti, L. *Growth and Income Distribution: Essays in Economic Theory.* Cambridge: At the University Press, 1974.

Patinkin, D. *Money, Interest and Prices.* New York: Harper and Row, 1965.

———. "Keynes' Monetary Thought: A Study of Its Development." *History of Political Economy*, Spring 1976.

———. *Anticipations of the General Theory.* Oxford: Blackwell, 1982.

Pigou, A. C. *The Theory of Unemployment.* London: Macmillan, 1933.

———. "Mr. J. M. Keynes' General Theory of Employment, Interest and Money." *Economica*, May 1936.

Ramsey, F. P. "A Mathematical Theory of Saving." *The Economic Journal*, December 1928.

Robertson, D. H. "Mr. Keynes' Theory of Money." *The Economic Journal*, September 1931.

———. "Some Notes on Mr. Keynes' General Theory of Employment." *The Quarterly Journal of Economics*, November 1936.

Robinson, J. "A Parable on Saving and Investment." *Economica*, February 1933.

———. *Freedom and Necessity.* London: Allen and Unwin, 1970.

———. "The Second Crisis of Economic Theory." *The American Economic Review.* Papers and Proceedings, May 1972.

Russell, B. *The Autobiography of Bertrand Russell.* London: Allen and Unwin, 1967.

Schumpeter, J. A. *Ten Great Economists from Marx to Keynes.* London: G. Allen and Unwin, 1952.

Shackle, G. L. S. *The Years of High Theory.* Cambridge: At the University Press, 1967.

—————. "New Tracks for Economic Theory, 1926–1939." In *Modern Economic Thought*, edited by S. Weintraub. Philadelphia: University of Pennsylvania Press, 1977.

Spaventa, L. "Realism without Parables in Capital Theory." In *Recherches recentes sur la fonction de production*. Centre d'Etudes et de Recherches Universitaires de Namur, 1968.

Sraffa, P. "Dr. Hayek on Money and Capital." *The Economic Journal*, March 1932.

—————. "Money and Capital: A Rejoinder." *The Economic Journal*, June 1932.

Tobin, J. "Money, Capital and Other Stores of Value." *American Economic Review*. Papers and Proceedings, May 1961.

—————. "A General Equilibrium Approach to Monetary Theory." *Journal of Money, Credit and Banking*, February 1969.

Vicarelli, F. "Disoccupazione e prezzi relativi: Un tentativo di reinterpretazione di Keynes." In *La controversia Keynesiana*, edited by Vicarelli (Bologna: Il Mulino, 1974).

—————, ed. *La controversia Keynesiana*. Bologna: Il Mulino, 1974.

Walras, L. *Elements d'economie politique pure*. Paris, 1926. Translated under the title *Elements of Pure Economics*. London: Allen and Unwin, 1954.

Weintraub, S. "A Macroeconomic Approach to the Theory of Wages." *The American Economic Review*, December 1956.

—————. "The Micro-Foundations of Aggregate Demand and Supply." *The Economic Journal*, September 1957.

—————. *An Approach to the Theory of Income Distribution*. Philadelphia and New York: Chilton Books, 1958.

—————. "Hicksian Keynesianism: Dominance and Decline." In *Modern Economic Thought*, edited by S. Weintraub. Philadelphia: University of Pennsylvania Press, 1977.

—————. *Capitalism, Inflation and Unemployment Crisis: Beyond Monetarism and Keynesianism*. Reading, Pa.: Addison-Wesley, 1978.

—————. "The Missing Theory of Money Wages." *Journal of Post-Keynesian Economics*, Winter 1978–79.

—————. "The Marginal Efficiency of Capital and Its Supply Price." *Journal of Post-Keynesian Economics*, Winter 1983.

Wicksell, K. *Geldzins und Güterpreise*. Jena: G. Fisher, 1898. Translated under the title *Interest and Prices*. London: Macmillan, 1936.

Wittgenstein, L. *Philosophische Untersuchungen*. Translated under the title *Philosophical Investigation*. Oxford: Basil Blackwell, 1953.

Young, A. "Increasing Returns and Economic Progress." *The Economic Journal*, December 1928.

Zaghini, E. *L'accumulazione di capitale*. Rome: Edizioni Ateneo, 1967.

INDEX

Aggregate demand: definition of, 119; determinants of, 150; and effects on output, 149; and *ex-ante* values, 166
Aggregate supply, 119, 124n.20
Animal spirits, 135, 138, 144

Bank of England, 10, 54, 63
Barter economy, 96, 99
Bolshevism, 17
Bradbury, Lord, 49
Bretton Woods Conference, 12
Brown, Ada Florence, ix

Cambridge "Circus," 101, 108
Cantillon, Richard, 72
Capital: accumulation of, and decision to save, 177; accumulation of, in Europe, 25; accumulation of, and social relations, 32; accumulation of, in Walras's theory, 161; markets, 9, 105; movements of, 9, 52; neoclassical theory of, 180
Cassel, Gustav, 88
Central bank: independent role for, 12; lack of, in India, 10
Chamberlain, Austen, 4, 12, 16, 20
Churchill, Winston, 49
Clemenceau, Georges, 19
Commons, John, 60
Communism: and economic effi-

ciency, 31; as new social order, 30
Credit: and banking system's neutral policy, 93; cycle, 75, 105; as determinant of interest rate, 166; rationing, 51n.6
Crisis, 80, 81, 99, 106, 137, 183, 184

Davis, Norman, 16
Deflation: and the debt burden, 151; and distribution of wealth, 36; and effects on savings, 35

Edgeworth, Francis Y., 118, 121
Effective demand: definition of, 120; and employment, 147; as essence of the *General Theory*, 165, 171; and interest rate determination, 162, 163
Employment: and aggregate demand, 149; and "bottle-necks," 153; effective level of, 121; general theory of, 177; long-run, level of, 179; in monetary economy, 146; multiplier, 109, 124n.20; primary and secondary, 109; as structural phenomenon, 155
Equilibrium: as classical "center of gravitation," 175, 176, 177; Hahn's notion of, 178; and in-

Post Keynesian Economics

Sidney Weintraub and Marvin Goodstein, eds. *Reaganomics in the Stagflation Economy*

Mark Obrinsky. *Profit Theory and Capitalism*

Fausto Vicarelli. *Keynes: The Instability of Capitalism*